TOWARDS THE CITY

❖❖❖❖❖❖❖❖❖❖❖❖❖❖❖❖❖❖❖❖❖❖❖❖❖❖❖❖❖

A version of Psalms 101–150

JIM COTTER

SHEFFIELD
CAIRNS PUBLICATIONS
1993

First published 1993

Further copies of this book are obtainable from
Cairns Publications
47 Firth Park Avenue, Sheffield s5 6HF

The first and second volumes in this series,
Through Desert Places, and *By Stony Paths*
are also available

*Printed by J. W. Northend Ltd
Clyde Road, Sheffield s8 otz*

CONTENTS

PSALMS 120–134: *The Pilgrim Psalms*

Contents

PSALMS 146–150: *Concluding Psalms of Praise*

PREFACE

THIS volume completes a series of new versions of the Psalms. The first, *Through desert places,* was inspired by Psalms 1–50, and the second, *By stony paths,* by Psalms 51–100. *Towards the city* looks at the last fifty psalms. (The three titles form three phrases in one, thus expressing something of the original spirituality of these ancient songs.) I would emphasise that these particular versions are neither translations from nor paraphrases of the Hebrew. Rather are they a new unfolding, the aim being to re-shape them so as to make them more directly prayable today. Weaving in and out of the original themes and prayers are images and experiences derived from the New Testament and from the twentieth century.

Each psalm is provided with a refrain and a final prayer. The refrain could be said corporately while the various sections could be said by solo voices. After the refrain has been said for the last time there could be period of silence during which particular intercession could be made for people who had come to mind during the reading of the psalm. Then the final prayer, reflecting the theme of the psalm, could be said by everybody present.

A more extended introduction to the three volumes is to be found at the beginning of *Through desert places.* The introduction to the second volume explores one of the most difficult questions that any religious faith has to explore, a question that exerts its pressure on us as we use the Psalms: How is it possible to reconcile belief in a loving God with the excessive amount and degree of suffering in the world? It does so by reflecting on the writings of Primo Levi, R. S. Thomas, and Margaret Spufford. The introduction to this volume looks at the insights of Francis Sullivan and Walter Brueggemann, who, as poets and scholars, have distinctive things to say about the Psalms.

I wish to express my thanks to all those who have used *Through desert places* and *By stony paths* and who have encouraged me by eagerly asking when *Towards the city* was going to be published. I have been warmed by their appreciation. And I am especially grateful to Lavinia Byrne for her Foreword to this book and for her critique of the draft manuscript of all three volumes.

I should also mention that a few of these versions have appeared in similar forms in the compilations *Prayer at Night* and *Prayer in the Day*. The prayers at the end of Psalms 107 and 136 echo, respectively, the Angel in Auden's *For the time being* and Dag Hammarskjöld's *Markings*.

The titles I have chosen suggest that the Psalms provide poems and songs for pilgrims on the journey to and into God, and towards a renewed community in a renewed creation. Indeed, the original title proposed for the second volume was *On pilgrimage*. (It was changed to *By stony paths* because 'pilgrimage' was too long a word for the cover design.) Within these last fifty psalms those numbered 120–134 have been particularly associated with the pilgrimage of the people of Israel 'going up' to Jerusalem. They are sometimes known as the 'Songs of Ascent', the ascent being to the gates of the city.

The long Psalm 119 is almost a collection in itself. It has its own character which reminds us not only of pilgrimage, but of the wisdom of God, the Law, the Torah, the Way, i.e. the whole counsel of the living God in covenant with the people. The twenty-two sections reflect this theme as if they were varying shafts of light from a crystal. In this book they are set out rather differently from the rest of the psalms. There is an introduction printed in italics, which could be read by a solo voice, followed by three lines, 'The journey', 'The invitation', and 'The implication'. The word or phrase on the first line suggests an event on the journey or a stage of the pilgrimage. The 'invitation' is from the Gospels, that of Jesus to the people among whom he lived. The 'implication' is a suggestion of how we might find ourselves responding if we take both journey and invitation seriously. Notice that these phrases are not explicit commandments in the sense of rules and regulations which must be mechanically obeyed in detail. Rather do they unfold for us certain characteristics of our lives which will become typical once we have responded to the gracious invitation of the living loving God. (Psalm 119 originally appeared in substantially this form in the book *Prayer in the Day*.)

So the Songs of Ascent and the Living Way, with their themes of a living pilgrimage and a living wisdom, are two of the major subdivisions of the last fifty psalms. There are two others which introduce us to a third way of looking at the Psalms, that they are songs of living praise. These are the Hallel Psalms (113–118 and 136), the name being derived from Hallel-Yah, Alleluia, Praise the Lord. They are traditionally associated with the Jewish Passover.

The second group of psalms of praise are the last five psalms, 146–150. These take up the myriad voices of the whole Psalter into a final harmony of joy and delight in God.

JIM COTTER
Sheffield, August 1993

FOREWORD

THE psalms are prayers; when we use them we learn how to pray. For this reason, in every generation, we are invited to turn to them in a new way, as a word given in our own time and addressed to our condition.

So what is the new way which Jim Cotter develops in this, the final collection, numbers 101–150, in his trilogy of Psalms? And what word in particular meets our concerns in this new book?

The new way is already familiar to those of us who have found fruitful material for prayer in his previous works. For it is the language, above all, which marks these out as a truly inclusive collection of prayers. And that does not simply mean that women and men may use them with equal confidence. It means that God too is named in ways which invite us to draw closer to the mystery which the Old Testament psalmist sought to disclose: the mystery which Christianity has consolidated by revealing to us the deepest desire of God, namely to be with us – and not apart from us.

And what in our condition invites us to pray these psalms with new authority and confidence? The newspaper headlines this week speak of war and rumours of war. Of the needs of the poor and undefended. Of fiscal controls and uncertainties which will dictate how world leaders will meet or fail to meet the great social and developmental needs of our times. As you use these psalms the same troubled world will scream to you from what you read in the press and see on your television screen or hear on your radio. A world in need will demand your prayers.

But there will be telephone calls as well, and letters and conversations in which people will ask that your prayers meet their need. Your families and friends and neighbours will name humble concerns: to match the exalted, global ones. And in deep and disturbing ways, you will know that plethora of unbidden thoughts and hopes and anxieties which bring you to pray for yourself.

The psalmists knew that real prayer does not shy off from concerns such as these. They form the matter of a faith-filled call upon the mercy, the graciousness and the anger of God. There is nothing precious about a real praying person. We pray from the real at our most authentic. And from the unreal at our most inauthentic. So when we rant and rage at God and dare to name what really concerns us, as opposed to what we think ought to concern us, we take the risk of faith which the psalms know by heart.

And when we find that we are too exhausted to care, or that words cannot convey what we are feeling anyway, then there is still something of substance here which will help us pray. For this is a book you do not have to finish. All you have to do is to use it in the confidence that the leap of faith and desire from the human heart is a leap of desire which is met by the heart of God.

LAVINIA BYRNE IBVM
London, August 1993

INTRODUCTION

SHOULD the words of Scripture be prayed only in the original language, or, as second best, in the most accurate translation? There are those who think so. When the first metrical versions of the Psalms were composed in Scotland, pains were taken to use only the words already on the printed page. Some competent verse was produced in this way, but there were more than a few tortuous constructions for the sake of the rhyme.

Others have thought differently. Perhaps the best known metrical version of Psalm 23 is 'The Lord's my Shepherd', often sung at funerals to 'Crimond'. The words are close to the original. But other versions make changes. H. W. Baker's hymn begins with a phrase not found in Psalm 23: 'The King of Love my Shepherd is'. It goes on to make more explicit reference to the New Testament in these lines,

> "Thy rod and staff to comfort me,
> Thy cross before to guide me."

Did Joseph Addison, English essayist of the eighteenth century, write his version. 'The Lord my pasture shall prepare', during a weekend at a friend's country house, set in a newly laid out park? After mentioning panting in 'the sultry glebe' – hardly the landscape the Psalmist would have been familiar with – we have these lines:

> "To fertile vales and dewy meads
> My weary wandering steps he leads,
> Where peaceful rivers, soft and slow,
> Amid the verdant landscape flow."

That version is not untrue to the spirit of the original psalm, but it is certainly a reflection of a different clime and age. Today it is probably sung by an English city-dweller with nostalgia for a vanished countryside, a nostalgia which conveniently forgets what rural life was like in the eighteenth century for most of those who worked there.

If the Holy Spirit has been promised to guide us into the truth, and the truth is not simply propositions but discovered in and among the lives of human beings in relationship, then we can expect new unfoldings in each generation, some of which will be criticised by the next. We may be in communion with our ancestors of faith, but surely not slavishly or uncritically. Indeed I would maintain that it is our responsibility to listen for and articulate fresh thoughts for a new day, reflections charged with the poetry and passion of our experience, bringing out treasure old and new from the scriptures and songs of the past and writing our own as well.

Walter Brueggemann, an American Lutheran scholar, has written a theological commentary called *The Message of the Psalms* (Augsburgh, 1984). He gives us a way of understanding the Psalms by a new classification. He warns that this is no newly discovered master-plan that has been hidden until now, but a different way of seeing, a perspective that may help us to appreciate what we otherwise might not have noticed.

Some psalms celebrate God's good blessings in ordinary life and God's wisdom and law. They are for settled times. Brueggemann calls them 'psalms of orientation'. Others, of complaint and grief, arise out of the experience of personal and communal dislocation – 'psalms of disorientation'. Then, in gratitude for God's deliverance, God's surprising saving action, there are the 'psalms of re-orientation'. He invites us thereby to enter more deeply into the psalms as they are and also to make connections between them and Christian and contemporary experience. The psalms of orientation he links to the continuities of Jewish life in countryside and towns, and to the incarnation of Christ. The breaking apart of a settled order he links to Jewish suffering, and to the crucifixion of Christ. The bewildering surprise of re-orientation he links to Jewish hopes of a new age, and to the resurrection of Christ. So we are encouraged to make our own connections between experience and expression in our present generation.

His list is not exhaustive, but here are the contents of his book, together with the numbers of the psalms he discusses in detail:

1 Psalms of orientation
    Songs of creation: 145, 104, 33, 8
    Songs of Torah: 1, 119, 15, 24
    Wisdom psalms: 37, 14
    Songs of retribution: 112
    Occasions of well-being: 133, 131

2 Psalms of disorientation
    Personal lament: 13, 86, 35
    Communal lament: 74, 79, 137
    Two problem psalms: 88, 109
    A 'second opinion': 50, 81
    The 'seven psalms': 32, 51, 143, 13
    After the deluge, Thou!: 49, 90, 73

3 Psalms of new orientation
    Thanksgiving songs: 30, 40, 138, 34
    Thanksgiving songs of the community: 65, 66, 124
    The once and future king: 114, 29, 96, 93, 97, 98, 99, 47
    Thanksgiving generalized to confidence: 27, 23, 91
    Hymns of praise: 117, 135, 103, 113, 146, 147, 148, 100,
        149, 150

Because of this variety in the psalms there will, at any one
particular time, be some which we cannot make our own. Hence
the suggestion that solo voices read the various verse sections
with the company saying only the refrains and the concluding
prayers.

Francis Sullivan has taken this idea further. He maintains that
half of the psalms cannot, as they stand, be prayed by the
Christian community. Now this is a more disturbing thought
than the encouragement Walter Brueggemann gives us to go
more deeply into them and make connections with our own
experience. Sullivan insists that we cannot directly pray the
brutal psalms. Of course we have such feelings and may be
tempted to act on them. These psalms can remind us of that, but
only if they are spoken by a solo voice. Otherwise they can too
easily become our own voice. They are also part of our common
past, our corporate memory, and they can remind us that we too
may fail to live up to our mature understandings of God.

"I would read (these psalms) as dramatically as possible and let them create the effects of passion and unease... A certain fear comes over me when I hear the complete psalter referred to as the prayer of the church. I fear the sword dance and ecstatic vengeance of Psalm 149. I fear the brain bashing of Psalm 137, the torture called for in Psalm 120, the slaughter right and left in Psalm 118, the curses of Psalm 109, whomever they belong to. I even fear the self-righteousness of beautiful 139. And on down to Psalm 2 where God, if angered, makes people perish and quickly. Maybe some psalms are the prayer of the church. Maybe others are its cross... When I pray in the name of Jesus, I have to pray for creation, or re-creation, or transformation, or straight-out mercy, or straight-out healing, or for forgiveness, or for union, or for companionship, or for straight-out love. I find it impossible to curse in the name of Jesus, even a fig tree, even those who destroy the souls of children, or those who twist religion into an instrument of personal power. I do pray for the pressure of the truth on such people and pray that the pressure be everlasting if need be, and that God be the truth that is the pressure." (*Tragic Psalms,* The Pastoral Press, 1987, pp. 203-204).

Sullivan has also published a second volume, *Lyric Psalms* (1983). There are seventy-five in each. Here is a list of the 'lyric psalms', those he would claim appropriate for communal prayer. (The number omitted here are of course the 'tragic psalms'.)

1, 4, 6, 8, 13–16, 19, 22–24, 26, 27, 29–34, 38–40, 42, 43, 50, 51, 65–67, 71–74, 77, 82, 85, 86, 88, 90, 91, 93, 95–98, 100, 102–105, 107, 111–117, 121–123, 126, 128, 130, 131, 133, 134, 142, 143, 145–148, 150

This kind of critical solidarity with our ancestors of faith can be illustrated in two other ways. The first is to take courage from the way in which we see that very process of reflective criticism at work within the psalms themselves. Psalm 51 gives a clear example. It is a deeply personal penitential psalm: the sacrifice that God desires is a humbled spirit and a contrite heart. But the two verses at the end of the psalm are so different in tone that they must have been added by a later hand. An official in the Temple? Well, somebody who, whilst conceding that the right *intention* was necessary in the worshipper, nevertheless affirmed that young bulls could then be offered upon the altar. We might want to ask a similar question, but with our own dilemmas in mind: Can the nonconformist (*my* way of praying) and the conformist (we must all pray in exactly the same words) give way to a variety of acceptable ways of praying within a common loyalty to one another, ways which are recognisably in continuity, however transformed, with the past?

Second, something painful is happening in our day which is bewildering not only to the conformists. Rather than being able to claim we belong to one overarching culture, even in one country we are getting used to moving from one subculture to another in a pluralistic society. How to foster the well-being of the whole community, global, regional, or local, with such diversity, is an acute question for our times. But it is increasingly clear that so much of what was once claimed as universal is not now experienced as such.

This new unfolding of the psalms is written by an ordained, English, middle class, educated man, with the cadences of the sixteenth and seventeenth century echoing almost physically in his mind. Through it, however, the language of the silenced finds some expression because of his roots in some of the first peoples of these islands and because of his experience of the struggles of a sexual minority to find a way of speech that gives meaning to their experience. So the contribution in these pages can only be partial and temporary.

It is offered as a form of prayer *for the time being*. It may be used by many or by a few: a writer has no way of telling in advance. It will fade sooner or later. It should certainly be challenged and changed: few contemporary prayers last beyond the generation in which they were written. We are in any case in a period of profound and rapid change. Those in science and theology who describe a 'paradigm shift' note that the emphasis is moving away from static unalterable forms and structures to a priority given to processes and relationships in a changing body of people as they reflect on their experience. Maybe we shall 'settle down' again one day to a widely accepted form of 'common prayer'. Maybe we shall recognize we belong to an 'ecumenical' communion by the acceptance of common values and principles, yet expect diversity of expression.

That we do belong to one another, through space and time, is now becoming more widely accepted. In Christian understanding this is reflected in language about the interdependent Body of Christ, a renewed, transformed creation, and the communion of saints. Our praying of the psalms can lead us more deeply into that reality: it is one reason why psalms and intercession have often gone together in their use. Indeed, the monastic daily office is largely built around those two impulses of praise and intercession that harmonise in the saying or singing of the psalms. When we cannot ourselves identify with a particular experience described in a psalm, we can make the saying of it into a prayer for those who can.

Maggie Ross has written of her sense of this communion in *The fire of your life* (Darton, Longman, & Todd, 1992), and it is with two quotations from that book that I would like to finish this introduction.

"Sometimes when I bow before the glory of God... I see from the corner of my eye, as mirrors reflect into other mirrors, an infinite line of shimmering figures bowing with me. Sometimes I see them *en masse,* as crowds are painted in early Byzantine art. Or sometimes I see a lone shepherd or hermit, voice roughened by years of singing against wind and sun, wandering in solitude...

They sang, sing, through nights and days, heat and cold, in home and hearth, desert and monastery, in dressing-gowns, skins, heavy wool, jeans, ornate great-schemas, leaning in the weariness of the small hours against a bed, a stone wall, a carved misericord, or, as I once did at midnight with a Cistercian friend, against the hard, plastic seats of the New York subway.

But now there is no day or night for them as they sing: their time-bound, time-hallowed music lingers with us, though we know there is no time, only motion and bending of space-time. Their density, their holiness, their heart-songs bend with us, bend the continuum, bend before the glory of God, with the glory of God..."

PSALMS 101–150

THE SINGLE EYE

Refrain: Pierce our hearts with the light of your love,
our minds with the sword of your truth.

Take from us, O God, the burden of pretence,
the lie that we and our leaders are just.
Let songs of wisdom sound from our lips;
keep self-righteousness far from our hearts.

So often we pretend to be innocent,
blameless and free of all guilt.
Open our eyes that we may see clear:
there is no escaping our crookedness.

So often we slander our neighbours,
afraid of their class or colour or creed.
Expose to the light the projections of our minds:
it is ourselves we should see in their mirror.

So often we are angry with the greedy and proud,
the arrogant who are deaf to the cries of the poor.
Keep our eye single; give us hearts that are pure,
lest we trample without knowing what we do.

So often we grumble at people with power,
calling them deceitful and corrupt in their ways.
Humble us all whose eyes are so blurred:
dishonest we are, we discern not the truth.

So often we fail to take account of our wealth,
the power of body, possessions, or talent.
May the light that shines from the eyes of the humble
burn out the corruption to which we are blind.

God of truth, hold before our eyes a vision of your commonwealth, your reign
of integrity and wisdom, justice and mercy. Give to those in public life
minds that are true and hearts that are compassionate. May they be humbled
by those who pass by.

RESURRECTION PROMISE

Refrain: *To the One who has disappeared,*
to the Presence we know as Absence,
we wave with the shreds of our faith,
Is the power of death overturned?

We live through a night of deep trouble,
of dreams that disturb, of collapse and decay.
We restore the façades of our heritage,
but within the meaning has gone.
Even the stones turn to dust,
as the beauty of the ages departs.
The lines of power strut the landscape:
the energy that feeds them fails.

The smoke of my days rises in the twilight,
curls in the air and is gone.
Already my bones blaze in the furnace,
reduced to the ash that soon they shall be.
My heart is scorched and shrivels,
pounded like grass in the summer heat.
The groans of my throat shrink to a croak,
my skin is glued to my bones.

Like a bird that is trapped by midwinter,
I find no food in the frozen waste.
Anxiously I look all around me,
afraid of the swoop of my enemies.
Chattering and restless I flit to and fro,
screeching through the desolate silence.
Exhausted, I limp through the snow;
I sink to the earth, shot through by the wind.

Slowly, steadily, I turn to you, my hope,
daring still to whisper your name.
Surely your heart moves with pity,
even to the grey streaks of my hair?

Your name has been known by my ancestors,
my children will seek and will find.
The nations will at last sing your praise,
the rulers of the peoples give you glory.

Your heart must surely hear the cry of the destitute,
you cannot despise your little ones.
The wounded you embrace with compassion,
you slide back the bolts of the prisoners.
Oh, it sounds so glib – though we say it in faith –
so nearly like vain repetition.
We desperately want to believe it is true,
that those yet unborn may give you the praise.

You have broken my strength before my time,
the very days cut short, their gift snatched away.
Soon I shall perish, and yet you endure,
my clothes become rags, yet your years never fail.
A comfort perhaps – but the children still die,
and the barren know nothing but dust.
Can the young Man who died give us hope?
The cry of the night be answered with joy?

Where is the language of words that catch fire?
Where is the wonder of a birth that is new?
Where is the savour of salt on the breeze?
Where is the bouquet of the freshest of wines?
Where is the confounding of the powers in the land?
Where is the community indifferent to threat?
Where are the alert, the wise and compassionate?
Where are the gifts whose giving does not end?

Your promises, O God, stand for ever, yet our hearts are torn when we see
them unfulfilled, even the crumbs of reassurance fail to fall, and we are
shrivelled by perplexity and doubt. Keep us faithful through our winter.
May the slender thread hold.

UNFATHOMABLE LOVE

Refrain: There is no end to your mercy,
enduring and infinite is your love.

From the deep places of my soul I praise you, O God:
I lift up my heart and glorify your holy name.
From the deep places of my soul I praise you, O God:
how can I forget all your goodness towards me?

You forgive all my sin, you heal all my weakness,
you rescue me from the brink of disaster,
you crown me with mercy and compassion.
You satisfy my being with good things,
so that my youth is renewed like an eagle's.

You fulfil all that you promise,
justice for all the oppressed.
You made known your ways to Moses,
and all the people saw your deeds.

You are full of forgiveness and grace,
endlessly patient, faithful in love.
You do not haunt us with our sins,
nor nurse grievances against us.
You do not repay evil with evil,
for you are greater than our sins.

As vast as the heavens are in comparison with the earth,
so great is your love to those who trust you.
As far as the east is from the west,
so far do you fling our sins from us.

Just as parents are merciful to their children,
so are you merciful and kind towards us.
For you know how fragile we are,
that we are made of the dust of the earth.
Our days are like the grass,
they bloom like the flowers of the field:
the wind blows over them and they are gone,
and no-one can tell where they stood.

Only your merciful goodness endures;
age after age you act justly
towards all who hold on to your covenant,
who take your words to heart and fulfil them.

For you have triumphed over the power of death,
and draw us to your presence with songs of joy.
We hear the echo of your angels praising you,
and the whole communion of your saints,
those who have walked in your narrow ways,
and heard the voice of your yearning,
whose food is to do your will,
and in whom you take great delight.

From the widest bounds of the universe
to the depths of my very being
the whispers and cries of joy
vibrate to a shining glory,
O God, our beginning and our end.

*Creator God, as we contemplate the vast universe of which we are so small
a part, swamping us with fear and despair and our insignificance, deepen
our trust that the profoundest meaning of it all is Love, beyond whose reach
it is impossible to fall.*

EXUBERANT WONDER

Refrain: Marvellous and vigorous,
splendidly unfolding,
the wonders of creation
we contemplate with awe.

Praise be to the Creator:
fresh energy divine,
with passion and with tenderness,
brings beauty new to birth.

Light from the dawn of the cosmos,
reaching out over billions of years;
the sun so familiar and steady,
spun off from that ancient fireball:
the primal explosion murmurs,
we hear the hiss of the aeons,
whispering insistent relic
of the original moment of time.
The beginning was all flame,
and the flame was unfurled into time;
all that has come into being
began at the heart of the flame.
Slowly the fire cooled,
the storm of particles ceased,
combed into structures of matter,
clouds and clusters of galaxies.
The cosmic dust was scattered –
a heart bursting into stars:
truly strange is our ancestor –
we ride on its pulsing still.   *Refrain*

Alone we seem in the darkness,
puppets of impersonal forces,
at best a mere flicker of light,
extinguished against the night sky.

But look at the world of the atom,
a minute yet infinite space,
where the unpredictable happens,
place of the improbably new.
Innumerable fragments that scattered
our consciousness begins to make whole,
mysteriously linked to our minds,
synapses by the billion in our brains.
Sounds stir through our bodies,
themselves fashioned by the stars,
bound up with the smallest particles.
Each of us seems like a universe.
Do we see deep in your mind,
more incredible still, our Creator?
To and fro have you ceaselessly woven
this web of matter and energy?   *Refrain*

We stand on a cliff top and watch,
gazing out over infinite seas,
whence our ancestors lately emerged,
obeying the call to a more complex life.
And still in the teeming oceans
swim the marvellous creatures,
the vital plankton sustaining them,
on which we also depend.
There go the whales and the dolphins,
even, it is rumoured, Leviathan,
that great monster of the deep,
the delight and sport of our God.
The heat of the sun draws the moisture
up from the seas to the turbulent skies,
where the winds blow the rain-bearing clouds
to fall on the mountains and valleys.
Thence spring the rivers and streams,
watering the brown of the earth into green,
quenching the thirst of the animals,
bearing the people in trade and in play.   *Refrain*

Refrain: Marvellous and vigorous,
splendidly unfolding,
the wonders of creation
we contemplate with awe.

Praise be to the Creator:
fresh energy divine,
with passion and with tenderness,
brings beauty new to birth.

The eyes of the satellites roam,
the soaring balloons hover,
the gliders smoothly range,
they see the mosaics of earth.
There in the tangle of rain forests
is the clicking of insects, the slither of snakes,
the screech of parrots, the blanket of rain,
and numberless species yet to be named.
There jostle the shining mountains,
lands of the long white clouds,
eagles soaring to their eyries,
snow leopards ruling the heights.
There ripple the sands of the desert,
where the barren flowers at the touch of rain,
where the fennec fox watches and listens,
through the deep silence that falls with the night.
The lions of the savannahs roar,
the cedars of Lebanon spread their branches,
the cattle graze in the pastures,
the cats curl up in the sun.   *Refrain*

We harvest the goodness of earth,
we reap the wheat and the maize,
we pluck the grapes from the vine,
the olives from the gnarled branches.
You give us an abundance to share,
the loaves of life for the table,
wine to gladden our hearts,
oil to lighten our skin.

Yet the sun can scorch the corn,
the lava snap the trees,
the hurricane flatten the houses,
the tidal waves and river floods drown.
The meteors hurtle through space,
the stars explode and vanish,
the violence our hearts abhor,
yet playing its vital part.
We may believe your Spirit created
and renews the face of the earth:
the destruction tempers our praise,
darkened by pain and perplexity.   *Refrain*

*Creator God, we celebrate a new unfolding of the universe this day, in us
and in everything around us. We listen to the silence and we hear the rustling
of our breath, the hum of engines, the cries of birds... We question and we
adore... we wonder... we trust...*

THE COVENANTS OF GOD

Refrain: Give praise to the God of the Promise,
who keeps faith with the earth for ever.

Let us give thanks to you, O God, and call upon your name;
let us tell among the peoples the things you have done.
We sing to you, we sing your praise,
and tell of all your marvellous works.
We exult in your holy name;
even in our seeking we are joyful in heart.
Let us seek your wisdom and strength,
let us seek the compassion of your face.
Let us call to mind the wonders you have done,
your marvellous acts and your discerning judgments. *Refrain*

Time was when we were but a few,
small in number and aliens in the land.
We wandered from valley to valley,
from one oasis and people to another.
Even then you protected us,
keeping at bay those who would harm us.
Then you called down a famine on the land,
and destroyed the bread that we needed.
But you sent on a man ahead of us,
Joseph who was sold into slavery,
whose feet the Egyptians fastened with fetters,
and thrust his neck into a hoop of iron.
He was tested to the limit by his captors,
until the time when his words proved true.
Then the pharaoh sent word to release him,
to become steward of all his household,
to order his officers at will,
and to teach his counsellors wisdom. *Refrain*

Then Israel came into Egypt,
and Jacob dwelt in the land of Ham.
There you made your people fruitful,
too numerous for those who opposed us,
whose hearts you turned to hate us
and deal deceitfully with your servants.
Then you sent Moses your servant,
and Aaron whom you had chosen.
Through them you worked your signs,
and your wonders in the land of Ham.
You sent darkness to cover the land,
the darkness of your ways that we do not understand.
You turned their waters into blood,
and the fish rose dead to the surface.
Their country swarmed with frogs,
even into the house of the pharaoh.
You spoke the word and there came swarms of flies,
and gnats within all their borders.
You sent them storms of hail,
and darts of lightning into their land.
You struck their vines and their fig trees,
you sent locusts to devour their crops.
Death and decay spread its misery,
even to the firstborn of each family.   *Refrain*

You brought Israel out with silver and gold,
and not one of our tribes was seen to stumble.
Egypt was glad at our going,
for dread of Israel had fallen upon them.
You spread out a cloud for our covering,
and fire to lighten the night.
The people asked and you brought us quails,
and satisfied us with manna from your hand.
You opened a rock so that the waters gushed,
and ran in the parched land like a river,
For you had remembered your holy word,
the promise to Abraham your servant.
So you led out your people with rejoicing,
your chosen ones with shouts of joy.

Refrain: Give praise to the God of the promise,
who keeps faith with the earth for ever.

You gave us the land you had promised,
and we inherited the toil of others,
so that we might keep the gift of your law,
and faithfully fulfil your covenant.   *Refrain*

So we remember our ancestors' story,
how they knew you as the God of the promise.
Out of your limitless love
you have chosen, O God, to be bound
with the limits of body and time
to the earth and all its people.
For you renew the covenants of old,
ever deepening your promise to love.
In the covenant of exodus from Egypt
you brought the people out of slavery.
In the covenant of Sinai with Moses
you gave shape and meaning to their lives.
In the covenant with Abraham and Isaac,
with Jacob and their descendants for ever,
you vowed your loyalty to them,
giving them the land of the promise,
and requiring the response of their hearts,
a steady will to trust and obey.   *Refrain*

You sustain your covenant with Noah,
with the living creatures of earth,
that never again will you destroy them,
with a flood laying waste to the world.
Your love is for the whole of our planet,
a vow of restraint and protection for ever.
Again and again you renew your promise,
putting a new heart and spirit within us,
through a covenant sealed by your blood,
your last will and testament for us.   *Refrain*

You demand no unthinking obedience,
a loyalty blind and correct.
You do not try to control us,
you seek the pledge of our wills and our hearts.
You are the One who endures our betrayals,
with a precarious and vulnerable love.
You keep faith with us and humble us,
and so renew us in hope.
You laid down the power of coercion,
and gave of yourself with generous love.
Our hearts burst out with gratitude,
in awe at the wonder of your goodness.
You have bound yourself to us – we belong to you,
and to one another – there is no way to escape.
Keep us responding in friendship and service,
giving and receiving your presence among us,
protecting those who are weak and in need,
trust deepening in sacraments of love.   *Refrain*

*In the mystery of Divine Love, we become gifts to one another, bound
together in the covenants of God. In the paradox of our free will and destiny
let us all embrace, choosing in friendship to share our being and becoming.
And with that divine love, and in the spirit of that love, let us promise to be
steady and reliable in our loving for ever, to work for our mutual well-being
and the cherishing of our earth, to honour one another as God's dwelling
place, and to keep loyal and full of faith, our life-day long.*

AS OUR ANCESTORS DID

Refrain: Open our eyes that we may see
the harm we have done in the world.
Open our ears that we may hear
your word of warning and mercy.
Draw us through the narrowest of gates
to the wide open space of the promise.

O God of our ancestors we praise you
for your goodness and mercy for ever.
We can but stammer our gratitude,
so marvellous and mysterious are your ways.
Only the just and humble of heart
can sound the depths of the story.
In remembering the times that are past,
renew us in penitence and hope.
Come alive in us with the power that heals
that we may share in your freedom and love.
Let your shalom spread over the land:
let us rejoice that we belong to you for ever.   *Refrain*

We disobey you as our ancestors did:
we act perversely and do what is wrong.
We are glad in our moments of freedom,
whenever you deliver us from Egypt.
But soon we forget the wealth of your love,
filled with fear of those who pursue us.
You clear our way through the quaking marsh,
parting the reeds for the fleet of foot.
Heavy with chariots our enemies sink,
and no one returns with their story.
Bowed down by oppressions of self and of others
we cry out for help and you throw off our burdens.
Light of step we go on our way,
rejoicing in your love and singing your praise.   *Refrain*

It takes but a moment to forget you,
we blunder along and wait not for your counsel.
We cannot face how empty we are,
and greed takes hold in the desert.
In our craving we put you to the test,
and you give what we say we desire.
But envy and bitterness seize us,
and the loathing we have for ourselves
we project on to those who are holy,
like Moses and Aaron of old.
Faction and quarrel spread unchecked,
we are secretly glad when our neighbours fall.
"Let the earth itself swallow them up;
let fire burn our rivals even as they sleep."　　*Refrain*

Many are the idols we have made as our gods,
golden calves of comfort and money.
Again and again we exchange your glory
for the pursuit of the utterly worthless.
So easily do we forget what you have done
to bring us out of enslavement.
We need the holy ones we scapegoat
who can bear the fierceness of your love,
the fiery anger that would consume us,
did Moses not stand in the breach.　　*Refrain*

We refuse to recognize the gifts that you give,
our faith in your promise evaporates.
We grumble and murmur in our tents
and refuse to listen to your voice.
You lift up your hand against us,
to scatter us through the wilderness,
our children losing their respect,
and vanishing far and wide.
We turn to the many false comforters,
wanting change without cost to ourselves.
Still do we eat the food of the dead,
though it is but ashes in our mouths.
We provoke you to anger by our foolishness,
and the body starts breaking apart.

Refrain: Open our eyes that we may see
the harm we have done in the world.
Open our ears that we may hear
your word of warning and mercy.
Draw us through the narrowest of gates
to the wide open space of the promise.

Plagues rage round the world,
and few there are with the courage
to sacrifice their own comforts and wealth,
like Phinehas to draw near to your presence,
taking to themselves the wraths and the sorrows,
standing firm as the beacons of hope.
And yes, we embitter our leaders,
who in turn become faithless and rash.
So Moses suffered for our misdeeds,
when you were angry at the waters of Meribah. *Refrain*

We did not destroy the inhabitants of the land.
Did you not command us to cleanse it?
Should we have dismissed them from our hearts,
making them less than human in our sight?
But we did not even stand up for your truths,
we sought to make ourselves acceptable to them.
We started to follow their customs,
mingling in family and marriage.
We were seduced into worshipping idols,
and snared into deeds still more cruel.
With bloodlust we butchered our children,
surrendering to the demonic within us.
So the rivers were defiled with blood;
we made ourselves foul by our deeds.   *Refrain*

No wonder your anger blazed,
so obtuse and wicked had we become.
It seemed that you loathed your own people,
for you gave us to the hand of our enemy.
The rule of the oppressor stifled us,
stripping us of value and dignity.

Though you rescued us many a time,
yet we fell once again in our evil.
Nevertheless you looked on our distress,
you heard the cry of our lament.
You remembered your covenant with us,
and relented in mercy and pity.
Before the very eyes of our enemies
your love kept working to free us.
Preserve us, O God, gather us together,
that we may reverence and praise you for ever.   *Refrain*

Did you command your people to destroy,
to commit even genocide according to your will?
Were their enemies so utterly evil
that not one of them deserved to survive?
Despite the rebellion of our ancestors
you spared them and graced them still.
Is your covenant only for a few who are favoured,
flourishing at the expense of the many?
Is not the pure race a dangerous myth,
an illusion that has never been real?
Did not your people misunderstand your call
to be special for service, not privilege?
Such old rigid thoughts are too proud,
too dangerous for our fragile earth home.
Your covenant is with all that you have made,
loving all creation through pain to its glory.
Your power, not almighty in magic,
neither capricious nor blind in its force,
will sustain and redeem your world yet,
withholding your fierce scalding fire,
refining in the heat of your love,
bringing out of evil unimaginable good.   *Refrain*

*May we never become so angry that we lose touch with compassion. May
we receive divine wrath only as an aspect of divine love. May we never lose
respect for other human beings, created in the image of God. May we be
empowered by the Spirit to overcome all desire to harm and all prejudice that
treats others as less than human. O God, make us and keep us Christlike.*

THE CRY FOR RESCUE

We give you thanks, O God, for you are gracious,
and your mercy endures for ever.
You bear the awful cost of our rescue,
redeeming us from terror and pain.
Even as the relentless winds of the universe
raged through the silence of the ages,
your heart was stirring to bring us to life,
to gather as gifts to one another.

You are with us through all our bewilderments,
through the impenetrable mystery of evil and pain,
redeeming our wastes and our sorrows,
hiding from us the glory to come.

Sometimes we are strangers on the earth,
wanderers with no room to call our own.
We go astray in the wilderness,
lost in the trackless desert.
The mists come down in the mountains,
we wander on the featureless moors.
Aimlessly stumbling in the forests,
we find no way to a city to dwell in.
Hungry and thirsty, our spirits sink within us;
we languish and collapse, ready to die.

Then we cry to you, O God, in our troubles,
and you deliver us from our distress.

You set our feet on a path we had not seen,
and you lead us to a place we can make as our own.

Let us praise you, O God, for your goodness,
your lovingkindness to the children of earth.
With nourishing food you have satisfied us,
you have slaked our aching thirst.

We sit in darkness and the shadow of death,
shackled by misery and affliction.
We are signs of a world ill at ease,
broken and distressed, hearts torn apart,
tossing to and fro in rebellion,
spurning the word of our own deepest good.
Our wits are blurred by our troubles,
under their weight we stagger and fall.
Shamed by our guilt, trembling with fear,
isolated and lonely, we find no one to help.

Then we cry to you, O God, in our troubles,
and you deliver us from our distress.

You break the chains that keep us imprisoned,
you lead us gently by the hand and into the sun.

Let us praise you, O God, for your goodness,
your lovingkindness to the children of earth.
You have shattered the doors of bronze,
you have snapped in two the iron bars.

When we go down to the sea in ships
or take to the air in great birds,
we are overcome with fear and with awe
at your wonders in the deep and in the skies.
For at your word the stormy wind arises,
lifting the waves of the sea,
stirring the turbulent clouds.
We are carried up to the heavens,
and down again to the depths:
we are tossed to and fro in peril,
we reel and stagger like drunkards,
our craftsmanship is all in vain.

Then we cry to you, O God, in our troubles,
and you deliver us from our distress.

Storms without and within cease at your word,
the waves of the sea and the air are stilled.
We recover our poise, panic leaves us,
we discover a presence that guides us through.

Then we are glad because we are at rest,
and you bring us to the haven where we would be.

Let us praise you, O God, for your goodness,
your lovingkindness to the children of earth.
At the gathering of the congregation your name be praised.
From the seat of the elders may you be glorified.

Yet again we turn to our foolishness,
caught in the cycles of disease and rebellion.
We turn away from the food that nourishes us,
even though we are brought to death's door.
We are caught in traps of poverty,
unable to move, hemmed in to despair.
We are bound by the scripts of our ancestors,
their sinewy subtleties holding us fast.

Then we cry to you, O God, in our troubles —
not always do you deliver us from our distress.

Your word of release sometimes heals us,
and we know we are saved from destruction.

It is hard to do more than whisper our thanks,
we lose hold of the mystery of your goodness.
Sometimes the helplessness in which we are caught
cries out in the night with no answering word.

The perplexity of your ways gives us pain;
we live between prison and freedom.
One day are the doors flung open,
only for others to close on the next.
You turn the rivers into beds of parched stones,
you dry up the springs of water.
You make the fertile land barren,
mirroring the drought of our goodness.
You fill the desert sands with water,
in the dry ground fresh springs emerge.
You bring in those who are hungry
to settle there and till the soil.
We plough fields, plant vineyards,
reap crops, graze herds.

We are blessed and our numbers increase,
yet the very next moment we seem cursed.
One day we are well content,
the next diminished again –
with plague, famine and war,
with stress in adversity and sorrow.
Even the powerful are brought low
and wander again in the desert.
And you raise up the poor from affliction,
making them strong in the land.

Only the eye of faith can discern your ways,
and even then they mightily puzzle us.
But let us be wise and ponder these things,
wisdom still finds her way to your praise.
Ever and again you protect and restrain us,
always with yet more gifts in store.
Let us therefore praise you, O God, for your goodness,
Your lovingkindness to the children of earth.

Keep us faithful, O God, trusting in your promise and power to rescue and
redeem. In the darker places of faith's journey help us to discern our freedom
in choosing what is difficult as if it were easy. For then we shall have faith
indeed, and even at the bleakest times we shall praise.

THE MAKING OF MUSIC

Refrain: *With the voice of song*
and the sounds of nature,
with the instruments of melody
and the strains of the heart,
with the discords let loose
and the cries unshaped,
we seek to make music,
the music of God.

May the instruments of music
come alive in our hands.
May the flute and the harp
sing the praises of God.
May the strings of my heart
make melody in the morning.
May the song of my soul
be echoed by the dawn.
While oppression weighs heavy,
and grief bows the heart,
let songs of consolation
lighten the load.
Beloved, you embrace the universe,
reaching the depths of our darkness.
The music of your glory shimmers,
your faithfulness ever its theme.
The earth and all its inhabitants
you orchestrate into beauty.
For however discordant we sound,
you are always creating new harmonies.   *Refrain.*

In the music of poetry and song,
in the laughter of highland streams,
in the melody of curlew and nightingale,
we are joined in praise of your beauty,
We relish the names of the rivers,
the mountains, the lakes, and the forests,
the villages, towns, and cities,
the countries that stir our hearts.
All of them make music to you, O God,
each one of them part of your vesture,
a theme in the symphony of praise,
the sound of their name giving you glory.   *Refrain*

The trumpet calls the army to war,
the horn gives warning to the city.
The drumbeat swells our pride,
our feet tap out in unison.
"With God on our side we will conquer."
Victory is sweet music to our ears.
The armies clash, the harmonies shatter –
can the screech of the dying sing your praise?   *Refrain*

Where now is the music of hope?
A new sound from the heart of our God?
Can the trumpet and horn caress,
can the beat of the drum make us dance?
Will the way of the Christ bear fruit
from seeds of non-violent passion?
Can the discords of evil be transformed
in the searing flames of your love?
Can the powers that harm be disarmed?
Is our love strong enough to contain them?
Then we would hear such harmonies
as the world can barely imagine.
We would know our place in the making of music,
our very need for enemies banished for ever.   *Refrain*

*In the music of lament and celebration, of loyalties and questioning, of love
and protest, of ballad and cantata, we seek to be your partners, Creator God,
in the weaving of the patterns of glory. Inspire us, guide us, transform us.*

AN ANGRY AND FEARSOME CRY

Refrain: In the hope that defies despair,
when goodness itself is paralysed,
and the voices of praise fall silent,
the stones themselves cry out,
the pitying creatures put us to shame,
the earth's ancient wisdom warns.

Let us speak out for the silenced,
giving voice to the voiceless.
Let the screams be uncorked,
and the bellows of rage resound.
The cry of the abused and violated
has far too long been unheard.
The ignorance of those uninvolved
colludes with the guilty and shamed,
all conspiring in silence,
their wounds festering unseen.   *Refrain*

The wealthy with bribes and corruption,
the fearful blackmailed to silence,
the lawkeepers twisting the evidence,
the advocates skilled in deceit and delay,
the ministers who can never be wrong,
establishments protecting their own,
the bullies hiding their cowardice,
the soldiers with permission to kill,
their mentors warping their minds
to think of the enemy as vermin,
the women a target for rape:
all fall under the cursing.
For the present we withhold God's blessing,
while refraining to crush in our turn.   *Refrain*

And the women cry out in pain,
and the men and the childen too:
The blood that flows cries out for revenge –
cursed be the violence of the strong.
The child howls in the lonely night –
cursed be the hand that bruised.
The woman lies sobbing on the floor –
cursed be the hard eyes and the unyielding stone.
The body that trusted lies rigid with shock –
cursed be the relishing of pain.
The weak are intimidated and afraid –
cursed be our arrogance and lust for power.
The abused shrink away in silent shame –
cursed be the evil power of secrecy.
The abusers protest their innocence –
cursed be the refusals and denials.
The comfortable turn away, refusing to see –
cursed be our collusion and cowardice.   *Refrain*

What is the voice of the dead-strewn streets?
Of the infants buried by rubble?
"Woe to you who work evil in the land,
inventors and makers of weapons,
automatic in the spattering of blood,
of semtex packed in a purse,
exploding in the face of passers-by.
Woe to the pride of your technology,
destroyers lurking in the city's cellars,
endemic to your way of death
from the hands of desperate men.
Woe to the wars of car bombs and missiles,
the buttons and triggers of a control so remote
from the travellers blown from the skies.

Refrain: In the hope that defies despair,
when goodness itself is paralysed,
and the voices of praise fall silent,
the stones themselves cry out,
the pitying creatures put us to shame,
the earth's ancient wisdom warns.

Woe to the traders in arms,
woe to the traffickers in drugs,
woe to the poisoners of minds,
woe to the serial killers,
woe to the men of cold eyes,
woe to the remorseless hearts,
woe to those with no pity."   *Refrain*

O Christ of angry compassion,
sweeping away the exploiters,
moved to speak out for the little ones,
drawing the sting of oppression,
lift up the crushed in spirit,
empower them to find their own voice,
to shame the violators to penitence,
to hope for the time of forgiveness,
to strengthen the rule of law,
to heap coals of fire on their heads,
the fire of love's wrath and desire
for justice and peace to be shared
in reconciliation and joy for ever.   *Refrain*

Holy and just God, receive the feelings of our outraged and wounded hearts.
Console our grief, melt our fear, lift the burden of our shame. Restrain our
desire for revenge, and channel the fierce energies of our anger in the service
of justice and truth.

POWER WITH SERVICE

Refrain: To those with power give wisdom,
the spirit of true understanding.

The oracles of old exalted the king
to stand at the right hand of God.
As priest and prince he was to rule
not by descent but by God's call.
The sceptre of power was placed in his hand,
to shatter the heads of his enemies.
Through him God routed the armies,
striding across corpses strewn in the way.

A strange world to us, faded from view,
kings riding out on horseback to conquer.
The wars of our time have tarnished the glory,
the rhetoric of God but masking our pride.
Arrogance and greed are the gods that we follow,
and even the wars we name holy or just
degrade those who wage them, reminding us all
how cruel and cold the world can become.

Yet as we dig deep in these words from the past,
we see a vision of those who would lead:
they lay on themselves the robe of the priestly,
willingly weighed down by the burden of service,
sacrificing self for the good of their land,
growing in discernment and wisdom.
They bring greater good from the conflicts around them,
and they heal the wounds of the people.

God of Wisdom, guide those in power with your Spirit of true counsel, that they may discern the course that is just, sacrificing themselves for the common good, not only of their own country but of the whole earth, laying aside all pride of wealth and status. And may we all find the courage to use whatever power we have.

THE HEARTBEAT OF GOD

Refrain: The heartbeat of God, the Amen of love,
faithful for ever, steady and sure.

My gratitude, O God, flows on,
like the deep and silent river,
I join in the stream of praise,
with your people gathered for worship.
We take our place in the Story,
re-kindled in the seasons' round.
We celebrate your mercies of old,
and your deeds among us today.

The great words resound in our ears,
we delight in the God who embodies them:
your glory and splendour and justice,
your beauty and grace and compassion,
your truth and faithfulness for ever,
your covenant of promise and life,
your creative and redeeming power,
your holiness, wisdom, and love.

Day by day you nourish us,
feeding us with sacrament and word,
slaking our thirst from the wellspring,
the waters that never run dry.
You renew your covenant each morning,
loyal to your promise for ever.
Awesome is your love for us,
steady over aeons of time.

In the fickleness of our will, in the doubtings of our minds, in the betrayals
of our hearts, we can scarcely believe in your steady presence through the
years. Startle us afresh. Take our breath away. Renew our trust.

OUR HATRED OF GOODNESS

Refrain: With the wealth of your generous love,
melt the ice of our hating hearts,
dissolve our envy and bitterness,
assure us that we are beyond price.

The spirit of hatred eats us alive,
gnawing away, draining our energy.
With what twisted and mocking delight
the innocent are corrupted, the gentle are scarred.

We accumulate the goods of this world,
"our wealth a reward for our virtue."
Yet we look down from a superior height,
despising the poor, increasing their burdens.

Never content with the possessions we have,
greedy for more, we harden our hearts.
Restless envy peers out from our eyes,
so cold, suspicious, and harsh.

Some of us turn our hatred within,
believing we have no worth of our own.
Cool disapproval drove us to despair,
and we kill ourselves by degrees.

Goodness incarnate was too much to bear,
showing us how crabbed and bitter we are.
The rage to kill rose in our throats,
a satisfaction hollow and bleak.

You took to yourself, Compassionate God,
all our hatred and spite.
You endured with a passion unbroken,
you left us with nothing but love.

Refrain: *With the wealth of your generous love,*
melt the ice of our hating hearts,
dissolve our envy and bitterness,
assure us that we are beyond price.

So you impel us to justice,
generous in giving, caring for others,
no longer grudging and grim,
able to share with no need to control.

Help us, just and generous God, not to project perfection on to those who
lead us, nor give others the illusion that we ourselves are perfect. May we
leave no room for envy and hatred, and no longer howl with glee when the
good let us down.

THE ENERGY OF COMPASSION

Refrain: Alleluia! We dare to give praise to God.

As the light of dawn struggles through the gloom,
as the sun filters through the morning haze,
as the weary stretch into another day,

As the noonday sun burns and does not relent,
as the pressure mounts on the brain,
as the elderly nod through the afternoon,

As the shadows lengthen and the day declines,
as the air cools around the homeless,
as a night of grieving looms,

As we grow angry at senseless violence,
as we cradle the wounded in our arms,
as we patiently repair the damage,

As the sloucher straightens his back,
as the poor rise up from the scrapheap,
as the barren at last conceive,

As Sarah, Rebekah, and Rachel give birth,
as Ruth follows Naomi to a new home,
as Rahab and Tamar find their place in the story,

As we seek to deepen our trust,
as we glimpse the power of compassion,
as we see the divine in the outcast,

As we remember the tales of our ancestors,
as we recall the moments of freedom,
as we renew our strength at its source,

Refrain: Alleluia! We dare to give praise to God.

As the Spirit of awe overtakes us,
as the depths of compassion overwhelm us,
as the glory and splendour overshadow us,

As we worship at all times, in all places,
as we lovingly relish the Name,
as the people sing with one voice.

*As we seek to discern how to bless you, O God of Power and Compassion,
in all the circumstances and through all the events of our lives, keep our anger
within bounds so that it does not destroy, and keep our caring truthful so that
we do not allow ourselves to be destroyed.*

THE GOD OF EXODUS

Refrain: Alleluia! We give praise to the God of rescue.

We are slaves of a pitiless ruler,
bowed down by an alien language.
We cry to you, O God, in our distress,
and you rescue us by your servant Moses.

We ourselves become your sanctuary,
the people with whom you dwell.
You call us to live in your image,
even as the One who shows us your face.

Even Nature responds with awe
at your power in acts of redemption.
The sea and the river retreat in panic,
the whole creation assists our rescue.

The mountains quake and the rocks splinter,
the sheep and lambs quiver with fear.
Amazement grips us as the scene unfolds,
this theatre which resounds with your presence.

Dance, O earth, at the appearance of God,
turning your anguish to a paean of praise.
Your rocks are turned into pools of water,
solid flint into a flowing fountain.

Nothing is fixed, nothing secure,
when you lead us into freedom.
The gods of nature crumble,
the noise of the powers is stilled.

O God, your greatness is awesome,
your incomprehensible grace in our rescue.
Our voices combine with those of the earth,
we give you the glory for ever.

Refrain: We give praise to the God of rescue.

For now the very earth herself is our home,
a secret not known to the powerful.
For our God was born in a cave,
and was killed cast out of the city.

You owned not a single possession,
and yet the whole world is yours.
Only the one who can never be exiled
is free at the last and always at home.

*With exuberant delight and a touch of fear we remember the stories of our
ancestors, and we rejoice in you, O God, for you are still the God behind all
the powers, with infinite compassion and grace rescuing us from all that
enslaves us. Call us out of our imprisonments. Rescue us. Lead us to
freedom.*

IDOLS AND THE LIVING GOD

Refrain: Alleluia! We praise the Beloved, God beyond gods.

It is not to our name that praise is due,
but to yours, eternal God of Love,
for you are faithful and kind and merciful,
surpassing us all in wisdom and care.

Our idols are silver and gold,
the gods of money rule in our land.
They have mouths and utter platitudes.
They have eyes and see not the poor.
They have ears but hear no cries of pain,
they have noses and keep themselves clean.
Their hands touch no one with love,
their feet never walk the streets.
Keep us from growing to be like them,
may we put no trust in possessions.

Renew our trust in you, O God:
give us courage to face our enemies.
You remember us and you bless us,
you bless all who hold you in honour.

Creator of the universe, God beyond gods,
you give us the earth to care for.
You are far beyond our imagining,
yet you bless each one of your little ones.

Those who are dead to your love do not praise you,
nor those who are gripped by one of the powers.
Keep our love and our freedom alive,
that we may praise you with joy and delight.

*Free us, redeeming God, from all that would hold us fast, from all the
addictions to which we could fall prey. Keep us compassionate and firm
with others and ourselves, that together we may inhabit a land of true
liberation.*

DEATH LOSES ITS STRANGLEHOLD

Refrain: Alleluia! Praise to the God in whom death is no more.

You have heard, O God, the strains of my distress,
even the silent crying of my heart.
I love you because your ear inclined to me,
I know you were there for me in the day of my trouble.

The cords of death entangled me:
the snares of the grave held me fast.
Tentacles wrapped themselves round me,
crushing me to anguish and pain.

Desperate for air I called out:
Help me. Deliver me. Rescue me.
My strength is sapped, my energy draining away.
With my last breath I cried out in panic.

In your healing compassion you came to me,
with the kiss of life reviving me.
At my very last gasp you held me,
you snatched me from the jaws of the grave.

You delivered me from the stronghold of death,
you wiped the tears from my eyes,
you saved my feet from stumbling,
and I walked free in the land of the living.

How can I ever repay you, O God,
for all the gifts of your gracious love?
I will lift high the cup of salvation,
and give thanks for your holy name.

From time to time you rescue me, O God,
by the skills of your people, by means unknown.
You come to me in the guise of strangers,
I am humbled by their willingness to care.

But what of the people who perish?
What of the children who are wasting away?
Can you save us through the days of our dying,
through the river of no return?

Yet you are the God not of death but of life,
no power can withstand the power of your love,
All that frightens us shrivels in your path,
the trail that was blazed by the Pioneer.

*Living Christ, decisive clue to the Love that has no end, renew in us the
steady hope that even the power of death cannot keep us from your presence.*

A QUIET MOMENT OF PRAISE

Refrain: Alleluia! We whisper our praise.

A fragment of prayer from the psalmist of old,
Let all the people praise the name of our God.
So now in a quiet moment of praise
our gratitude whispers on the gentlest of breaths.

Not always with jubilant shouts
do we sound our thanksgiving and joy.
From the depths of a silent heart
comes a word but softly spoken.

Secure in the lovingkindness of God,
knowing the Love that always endures,
transforming the evils we face into good,
we waft the breeze and adore.

O God of Silent Loving, keep us from the trap of believing that the louder we shout the more genuine is our faith and the more fulsome is our praise. Keep us aware that love is fragile and vulnerable and that we know it best in the silence of the heart.

THE MERCIES OF GOD ENDURE

Refrain: Alleluia! We give thanks for the mercies of God.

Let us give thanks for the goodness of God,
let the people of old shout their joy.
Let the children yet unborn hear its sound,
the harmony of a people of praise.

In the dangers we face you are with us,
you came as one of us and set us free.
We need you no longer on our side,
for your love has spread over our enemies.

Yes, I long for the downfall of those who oppress me:
with the ache of sorrow I remember their harm.
But my bitterness has warmed to compassion,
my anger channelled for justice.

I take my refuge in your presence, O God,
putting no trust in rebellious powers.
The mighty of the earth are not worthy:
humble them to a place of repentance and trust.

When all the powers surrounded me,
in your name I drove them back.
When they swarmed around me like bees,
in your name I drove them back.

I was pressed so hard that I almost fell,
but your power surged through my arms.
For you are my strength and my song,
and have become my salvation and rescue.

So we bound up the rebellious powers,
and gave them into your care.
Take from them their desire for revenge,
and heal their deepest hurts.

Refrain: Alleluia! We give thanks for the mercies of God.

No one shall die and be forgotten,
not one of the little ones is lost.
If the hairs of our heads are numbered,
who can doubt the compassion of God?

We shall not die but we shall live,
and rejoice in the deeds of our God.
Even though you test us to the limit,
you do not abandon us to death.

Open for us the gates of the city,
the city of harmony and peace.
Together restored we enter them,
singing our songs of thanksgiving.

The stone which the builder rejected
has become the head of the corner.
The very ones we despised
are known as your specially beloved.

This is the festival day,
the day you have made for our joy.
We shall be glad and rejoice,
feasting with laughter and song.

Blessed are those who journey in your name:
the light of our God has guided them.
They join the throng in the places of praise:
indeed you are God: we adore you.

*May we not be stingy in our gratitude nor grudging in our praise. Loosen
our stiff bodies to be exuberant and joyful. Let us dance with delight and see
the sparkle in the eyes of God.*

WALKING IN GOD'S PATH

[*God's invitation to us is to follow Christ. It is a journey into Love, along a path that is rarely smooth. The Way is rough, the Truth is costly, the Life is sacrificial. The gate through which we are drawn by Love is always narrow.*]

The journey	The stony road
The invitation	Follow the Way, the Truth, the Life
The implication	Enter by the narrow gate

Blessed are those who are honest in their ways,
who walk in the paths of God's Law.

Blessed are those who treasure God's Wisdom,
who seek God with all their heart.

Those who do no evil deeds
are those who tread the way of Justice.

Dear God, you have given command
that we diligently hold to your Word.

May my ways be kept steadfast
on the narrow road of your Love.

So I shall not be confounded
while I respect the whole of your Counsel.

I shall thank you with unfeigned heart
as I learn to be guided by your Spirit.

I shall hold fast to your Truths:
do not utterly abandon me.

DELIGHTING IN GOD'S WISDOM

[*The path is tough, and, despite boundary marks, we wander from it. We become self-centred; we ignore others on the path. We are constantly invited to love others as Christ has loved us: that degree of love is not easy for it challenges us to bless, pray for, and help those who are hostile to us.*]

The journey	Boundary marks
The invitation	Love one another as I have loved you
The implication	Do good to those who hate you
	Bless those who curse you
	Pray for those who abuse you

How shall the young find their way?
By guarding the boundary of your Word.

With my whole heart I have looked for you:
let me not wander from your Commandment.

Your Truth have I hidden within my heart,
so that I should not fail to love you.

You are blessed indeed, dear God:
teach me your Wisdom.

With my lips I have been telling
of all the Judgments of your mouth.

I have had greater delight in the ways of your Loving
than in all manner of riches.

I will dare to contemplate your Countenance,
and I will deeply respect your Ways.

My delight will be in your Counsel,
and I shall not forget your Word.

LONGING FOR GOD'S JUSTICE

[*As travellers into God we need guideposts which can be discerned from within the words of the Gospels. For example, we are blessed when we hunger and thirst for the right relationships longed for by a just God. Only by being faithful to such wisdom will our lives be built on rock.*]

The journey	Guideposts
The invitation	Be faithful to what I have said
The implication	Build on rock

Deal bountifully with your servant,
that I may live, and keep your Word.

Open my eyes that I may see
the wondrous things of your Law.

I am a traveller upon earth:
hide not your Guideposts from me.

I am consumed with a very fervent desire,
a longing that I have for your Justice.

You have rebuked the pride that lurks in me,
you rescue me when I am lost and astray.

Take away from me the spirit of scorn,
hold me fast to the rock of your Truth.

Keep me from suspicion and hatred:
rather may I meditate on your Counsel.

For your Sayings are my delight,
and they are my counsellors.

ENDURING IN GOD'S WAY

[*When the way is dusty and hot, it is easy to feel weighed down and oppressed. We have then to stop and dig deep in the desert until we discover springs of refreshing water. We also need to learn to receive nourishment from other travellers, as much as in our turn give to them.*]

The journey	Water
The invitation	Let living water flow in you
The implication	Feed the hungry
	Give water to the thirsty

My soul is weighed down like lead:
revive me according to your Word.

When I told you of my ways, you heard me.
Teach me your Wisdom.

Help me to understand the Way of your Love,
and to meditate on the wonders of your Deeds.

My soul droops for very heaviness:
refresh me according to your Promise.

Take from me the way of lying,
and graciously teach me your Truth.

I have chosen the way of faithfulness,
and your Justice is before my eyes.

I cleave to your Law:
let me not be put to shame.

I shall run the way of your Commandment
when you have set my heart at liberty.

DESIRING LIFE IN GOD'S SPIRIT

[*We are called simply to follow, but with deep desire and not with reluctance. It is not a path of human cleverness, but of the Spirit of Wisdom. So we are to turn our eyes from envy of others' success, and turn them towards those who are needy.*]

The journey	Following
The invitation	Receive the Holy Spirit
The implication	Give to everyone who asks you

Teach me, dear God, the Way of your Truth,
and I shall follow it to the end.

Give me understanding, and I shall keep your Law,
I shall keep it with my whole heart.

Lead me in the path of Wisdom;
to do your Will is my deepest desire.

Incline my heart to your Love,
and not to envious greed.

Turn away my eyes from vanity,
and give me life in your Spirit.

Establish me in your Promise,
be faithful to those who are in awe of you.

Take away from me the rejection that I fear,
for your Justice is good.

See, my delight is in your Commandment:
quicken me in the power of your Word.

KEEPING GOD'S WORD

[*To keep on being steadily steadfast in God's Truth even when afraid of the powerful — this is to walk in a sacred manner. It is possible only if we dwell in God's Love. We shall be so delighted in God that we shall not even want to condemn those who would harm us.*]

The journey   Walking

The invitation   Abide in my love

The implication   Judge not and you will not be judged
Condemn not and you will not be condemned
Forgive and you will be forgiven

Let your steadfast Love spread over me, dear God,
even your salvation, according to your Promise.

So shall I have an answer for those who taunt me,
for my trust is in your Word.

Take not the Word of your Truth utterly out of my mouth,
for my hope is in your Justice.

So shall I always keep your Law,
for ever and ever the ways of your Love.

And I shall walk at liberty,
glad to fulfil your Commands.

I shall speak of your Wisdom and not be ashamed,
even among the powerful of the earth.

My delight shall be in your Counsel,
which I cherish with joy.

I shall lift up my hands in your Presence,
and listen deep within for your Word.

REMEMBERING GOD'S PROMISE

[*We go astray from the path. We pursue wordly wealth at others' expense, we despise the weak, we even betray friends. To remember God's Promise to be with us always, to ask that we may embody the Spirit of Christ, to contemplate and treasure Wisdom: only so do we renew our pilgrimage.*]

The journey   Astray

The invitation   Ask in my name

The implication   Do not lay up for yourselves treasure on earth

Remember your Promise to your servant,
in which you have caused me to put my trust.

It is my comfort in time of trouble,
for your Word has given me life.

In pride we despise one another:
may we not shrink from your Law.

Let us remember your Justice, O God,
and we shall be strengthened.

May my anger be cleansed by your Truth,
as I confront betrayal and wrong.

Your Sayings have been my songs
in the house of my pilgrimage.

I have thought upon your Name in the watches of the night,
and I have treasured your Wisdom.

It has been for my blessing,
when I have lived by your Commandment of Love.

ENJOYING GOD'S PRESENCE

[*We are enlivened and encouraged on the journey by companions — literally those with whom we eat bread. Even the stranger is to be welcomed as one who also belongs to God. We are to taste and see the goodness of the One who gives us living bread.*]

The journey	Companions
The invitation	Eat of the Living Bread
The implication	Welcome the stranger

Dear God, you are my portion for ever:
I have promised to live by your Spirit.

With heart and longing I come into your Presence:
show me your steadfast Love, according to your Word.

I call your Truth to remembrance,
and turn my feet to your Way.

I make haste, and prolong not the time,
that I might keep your Commandments.

The cords of the ungodly ensnare me:
may I not forget your Law.

At midnight I will rise to give you thanks,
because the Judge of all the world acts well.

I am the companion of all who are in awe of you,
who are guided by your Counsel.

The earth, O God, is full of your steadfast Love:
O teach me your Wisdom.

RECEIVING GOD'S GRACE

[*Fortified by God and by one another we journey on. Knowing that we are accepted as we are, we can the more readily accept and forgive others. We have received the gracious and truthful presence of God, far more enriching than all the world's wealth.*]

The journey	On course again
The invitation	Forgive the sins of others
The implication	Forgive to seventy times seven

Dear God, you have given me grace,
and so fulfilled your Promise.

Teach me true understanding and knowledge,
for I have trusted your Word.

Before I was afflicted I went astray,
but now I keep your Counsel.

You are good and gracious:
O teach me your Wisdom.

Through pride I tell lies against my neighbour:
keep me to your Truth with my whole heart.

My heart grows fat and gross:
let my delight be in your Love.

It is good for me that I have been afflicted,
that I may learn your Wisdom.

The Sayings of your mouth are dearer to me
than thousands of gold and silver pieces.

LETTING BE IN GOD'S HANDS

[*We are misled if we think our hard travelling earns us anything as of right.
We have to take time to stand still and do nothing, to let go of our concerns,
and to let be in God's hands, simply to trust and be thankful.*]

The journey	Standing still
The invitation	To do the work of God is to believe in the One whom God has sent
The implication	Hold on to your life and you will lose it Let go of your life and you will find it

Your hands have made me and fashioned me:
give me understanding that I may know your Mind.

Those who fear you will be glad when they see me,
because I have put my trust in your Word.

I know that your Judgments are right,
that in your faithfulness you have caused me to be troubled.

Let your merciful kindness be my comfort,
according to your Promise to your servant.

Let your loving mercies come to me, that I may live,
for your Love is my delight.

Let my pride be confounded, with its twists of deceit,
and I will meditate on your Wisdom.

Let those who fear you turn to me,
that they may know your Truth.

Let my heart be found in your Counsel,
that I may not be ashamed.

CLINGING TO GOD'S FAITHFULNESS

[*The vision with which we started out seems to shrivel. Eyesight and insight grow dim. We harm rather than help one another. At best we doggedly endure, clinging to the faithfulness of God who encourages us with Christ's victory over all that would drag us down. Feeling stripped to the bone, we are yet called to clothe one another.*]

The journey   Stumbling

The invitation   Be of good courage: I have overcome the world

The implication   Clothe the naked

I faint with longing for your salvation:
with hope I still cleave to your Word.

My eyes grow dim with watching for your Promise,
saying, When will you comfort me?

For I am like a wineskin shrivelled in the smoke,
yet I do not forget your Wisdom.

How long must your servant endure?
When will you judge those who oppress me?

Yet I too have laid traps for others,
and I have not obeyed your Law.

All your Commandments are true:
they challenge our falsehoods and deceit.

We have almost made an end of ourselves upon earth:
draw us back who have forsaken your Way.

Quicken me in your loving kindness:
and I shall keep the Counsel of your Spirit.

TRUSTING IN GOD'S PURPOSE

[*In the very midst of constriction the vision is renewed. Sustained by the
eternity and reliability and promised fulfilment of the purpose of God's
Love, nourished by the blood-red wine of the very life of God, we continue
to walk with our burdens, simply following the Way.*]

> *The journey*   Vision
>
> *The invitation*   Live in the True Vine
>
> *The implication* Take up your cross and follow me

Dear God, your eternal Word of Love
endures for ever in the universe.

Your Truth stands fast from one generation to another:
you have laid the foundations of the earth, and it abides.

In fulfilment of your Purpose it continues to this very day,
for all things serve you.

If my delight had not been in your Wisdom,
I should have perished in my trouble.

I shall never forget your Truths,
for with them you have given me life.

I belong to you, save me,
for I have sought your Counsel.

Many are the traps that could destroy me,
but I will meditate on your Law.

I see that all things come to an end,
but your Commandment is exceeding broad.

LOVING GOD'S TRUTH

[*We miss our way if we do not become childlike in our trust and delight in the tastiness of God's gifts. Even the commandment to love in a tough, enduring, non-possessive way is as honey to our deepest selves. We come to relish the Wisdom, Counsel, and Truths of God.*]

The journey	Honey
The invitation	If you love me keep my commandment
The implication	Become like children

Dear God, how I love your Wisdom:
all day long is my study in it.

Your Counsel makes me wiser than my adversaries,
for it is always in my heart.

I have more understanding than my teachers,
for I meditate on your Word.

I am wiser than the aged
because I keep your Truths in my heart.

I hold back my feet from evil ways,
that I may obey your will.

When I do not turn aside from your Way,
I know that you are my Guide.

How tasty are your Sayings to my mouth,
sweeter than honey to my tongue.

Through your guidance I learn understanding:
therefore I hate all evil ways.

BEING GUIDED BY GOD'S LIGHT

[*The Way becomes obscure, but there is sufficient light once our eyes are accustomed to the dark. We may not realize that we are being guided in a particular direction, but the shepherd's crook is kindly prompting. We may be troubled, but an imperceptible inclination of the heart in prayer is all that is needed for our calming.*]

The journey	Lantern in the dark
The invitation	Let the Good Shepherd guide
The implication	Pray simply

Your Word is a lantern to my feet,
a light searching out all my ways.

I have sworn, and am steadfastly purposed
to keep the Way of your Justice.

I am troubled beyond measure:
give me life, dear God, according to your Promise.

Accept my offerings of praise,
and teach me your Truths.

My life is always in your hands,
and I do not forget your Law.

The ungodly have laid a snare for me:
may I not swerve from your Commandment.

Your wisdom have I claimed as my heritage for ever,
it is the very joy of my heart.

I incline my heart to your Counsel,
always, even to the end.

BRINGING EVIL TO GOD'S JUDGMENT

[*We try to avoid the refining fire of God's truth. We resist the pruning of our self-centredness. We are unfaithful to our promises, we are cunning in our self-deceits, we become weighed down with our vain pursuit of earthly security. Even while hating hypocrisy, we practise it. Only through the astringent love of God will our greedy and inordinate desires cease, our lust for possessions fade.*]

The journey	Refining fire
The invitation	Be pruned, and be fruitful
The implication	Do not look lustfully

I hate all doublemindedness and hypocrisy,
but your Law do I love.

You are my defence and my shield,
and my trust is in your Word.

Away from me, all desire to do evil:
I will keep the Commandment of my God.

Uphold me according to your Promise, and I shall live:
let me not be disappointed of my hope.

Support me, and I shall be safe:
my delight shall ever be in your Wisdom.

Relentlessly expose my unfaithfulness;
may my cunning be in vain.

Rake out ungodliness from me like dross,
for I desire your refining Truths.

My flesh trembles in awe of you,
and I am afraid of your Judgments.

SERVING GOD'S WILL

[*As servants of the will of God, called to love God's wisdom as a precious
jewel, we begin to discover that indeed possessions are of no account. We
appreciate the wealth that comes to us through enjoying the smallest and
simplest acts of kindness, given and received. No earthly greatness could ever
compensate for such true treasure.*]

The journey	Possessions of no account
The invitation	Wash one another's feet
The implication	Whoever would be great among you must be your servant

I have done what is just and right:
do not give me over into the hands of my oppressors.

Make your servant delight in all that is good,
that the proud may do me no wrong.

My eyes waste away with looking for your salvation,
for the fulfilment of your righteous Promise.

Embrace your servant in your steadfast Love,
and teach me your Wisdon.

I am your servant: give me understanding
that I may know your Counsel.

It is high time that you acted, O God,
for your Law is being destroyed.

How I would come to love your Commandments
beyond all gold and precious stones.

Therefore I direct my steps in your Way,
and all false steps I utterly abhor.

REJOICING IN GOD'S LOVE

[*God's Love is reliable, steadfast, constant. In that knowledge we can walk firmly, freed from the weight of oppression, with a light step. Even in frightening places, it is as if we are already in the safety of the sheepfold. Living in the spirit of that freedom, we are more able to draw alongside those who are constricted by illness or imprisonment.*]

The journey	Burdens fall away
The invitation	Come in by the Door of the Sheepfold
The implication	Visit the sick and those in prison

Your steadfast Love is wonderful:
therefore I treasure your Wisdom.

When your Word goes forth
it gives light and understanding to the simple.

I opened my mouth and drew in my breath,
for my delight was in your Counsel.

Look upon me and show me kindness,
as is your joy for those who love your Name.

Keep my steps steady in your Word,
and so shall no wickedness get dominion over me.

Relieve me from the weight of oppression,
and so I shall keep your Commandments.

Show the light of your face upon your servant,
and teach me your Way.

My eyes shed streams of sorrow
because folk heed not your Promise.

THIRSTING FOR GOD'S JUSTICE

[*Freed from the weight of worldly expectation and possessions, humbled and poor, even, like a grain of wheat, dying unnoticed, the followers of the Way are the only ones who can know what it would be like to see God's justice, God's commonwealth, established on earth. They cry with yearning to see right prevail. They strive to make it so.*]

The journey   Humbled and poor

The invitation   Let the grain of wheat fall into the earth and die

The implication   Yearn and strive to see right prevail

You are righteous, O God,
and your Judgments are true.

The Ways that you have commanded
are just and true.

My zeal has consumed me
because my enemies have forgotten your Words.

Your Promise has been well tested,
and your servant loves and delights in it.

I am small, and of no reputation,
yet I do not forget your Wisdom.

Your righteousness is an everlasting righteousness,
and your Law is the Truth.

Trouble and heaviness have taken hold of me,
yet my delight is in your Justice.

The righteousness of your Will is eternal:
give me understanding, and I shall live.

URGENTLY NEEDING GOD'S GUIDANCE

[*Nevertheless, it is not easy to keep our sense of spiritual direction. We are easily misled and we have to face the malice of the frightened. We shall lie awake at night, seeking to settle our hearts and wills on God. We shall urgently pray for guidance in the day. We may be given the gift of God's peace, but we shall do well to strive with our enemies sooner rather than later.*]

The journey Awake at night

The invitation Receive my gift of peace

The implication Make friends quickly with your adversary

I call with my whole heart:
hear me, O God, I will keep your Commandments.

Urgently do I cry to you:
help me, and I shall follow your Way.

Early in the morning do I cry out to you,
for in your Word is my trust.

My eyes are awake in the watches of the night,
that I might meditate on your Promise.

Hear my voice according to your steadfast Love,
quicken me, in fulfilment of your Will.

They draw near who persecute me with malice:
they are far from your Law.

But you, O God, are near at hand:
for all your Counsel is true.

Long since have I known of your Wisdom,
that you have grounded it for ever.

CHERISHING GOD'S COMMAND

[*Not one of us can plead innocence or perfection. There is great contrast between our unfaithfulness and the steadfast love of God. This is painful truth. Only by immersing ourselves in God's Love, only by sharing the cup of affliction which was drained to the full by the only One who was indeed whole, can we be given the life that we desire. On the way we have to deny ourselves much of what we now hold dear.*]

The journey	Aware of painful truth
The invitation	Drink the Cup
The implication	Deny yourself

Look on my affliction and deliver me;
may I not forget your Law.

Plead my cause and redeem me:
give me life according to your Word.

Salvation is far from my wickedness,
when I have no regard for your Commandments.

Great is your loving kindness, dear God:
give me life, for such is your joy and delight.

There are many who trouble me, my adversaries:
may I not swerve from your Way.

It grieves me to see our unfaithfulness
when we ignore all that you promise.

Consider how I cherish your Wisdom:
give me life, according to your steadfast Love.

Your Word is eternally true,
and your Justice stands fast for ever.

STANDING FIRM IN GOD'S COUNSEL

[*If we keep to the Way shown to us, we shall discover the treasures of the Wisdom of God—Love, Truth, Peace, Saving Health, Justice. We are invited to trust and not be faithless, to open all the devices of our locked hearts to God. Then we shall be at peace, be able to absorb and reconcile conflicts, and be makers of peace.*]

The journey	Treasure discovered
The invitation	Be not faithless but believing
The implication	Be a maker of peace

The powerful oppress me without cause,
but my heart stands firm in awe of your Word.

I rejoice in your Love
more than one who finds great spoils.

As for lies, I hate and abhor them,
but your Law do I love.

Seven times a day do I praise you
because of the Justice of your Way.

Great is the peace of those who treasure your Wisdom:
nothing can make them stumble.

I have looked for your saving health,
and followed your Counsel.

My whole being holds fast to your Justice,
which I love and long for exceedingly.

Guide me in the path of your Truth,
all the ways of my heart are open before you.

PRAISING GOD'S SALVATION

[*The journey is through a labyrinth. We find our way to our true home by the thinnest of threads. Like bewildered sheep we lose our way in cul-de-sacs of the maze. If we have been found there by the 'angels' of God, then we in turn can at times be a 'presence' of God to others who are confused. In dark and hidden places we can still give, and pray, and fast. And in the end we shall be brought home rejoicing in the God who saves, in and through and beyond our hopes and fears.*]

The journey	Home through the labyrinth
The invitation	Feed my sheep
The implication	Give secretly
	Pray secretly
	Fast secretly

Let my cry come to your ears, dear God:
give me understanding, according to your Word.

See the labyrinth of my ways:
deliver me, according to your Promise.

My lips shall tell of your praise,
for you show me the path of Wisdom.

My tongue shall sing of your Love
and praise your Justice to the skies.

Let your hand guide me,
steady me with the Counsel of your Spirit.

I have longed for your saving health, O God,
and in your Truth is my delight.

Let me live, that I may praise you:
let your Love and your Justice help me.

I have gone astray like a sheep that is lost:
seek your servant, and bring me home rejoicing.

HELP AND HARM

Will I ever be free?

Refrain: Trapped and besieged,
unable to move,
I cry from my prison,
Let my journey begin.

From the days before I knew there were days,
in the darkness of continuing night,
I was caught in an alien country,
my enemy the source of my life.

Bewildered by the smiles of welcome and peace,
nourished, it seemed, for my good,
I lay close to pretence and deceit,
seen only in the light of another's esteem.

I breathed the air of whispered betrayal,
entangled as I was in the voice of the lie.
Infected by words that were bitter and sharp,
it was hard to resist the desire for revenge.

Like a fledgling my whole being trembled,
shaken by my first faltering steps.
At last I could leave the place of my peril,
glimpsing your love which is true and assured.

So you gave me the beginnings of freedom, O God:
the arrows will turn back on those who pursue me,
the burning of the broom tree will shrivel the lie,
my betrayer's heart seared to life by the truth.

Give me courage, Pillar of Flame, as I begin to follow you on the pilgrim
way. Create a calm and glowing centre within me that I may resist the
cruelties of those who seem to love me. May I be firm in refusing all
collusion. May I be harmed no more. Keep my steps steady when I arouse
unresolved conflicts within those with whom I seek to be reconciled. And free
them from their prisons too.

REFRESHMENT AND RIGOUR

Have I the courage to trust?

Refrain: Companion on my journey,
Protector at my side,
I venture on the way
in simple childlike trust.

I look towards the mountain ranges,
and fear their lurking terrors.
The pilgrim path takes me through them,
by rocks and ravines, ambush and vultures.
Stormy winds swirl round the summits,
avalanches threaten across trackless screes.
The hills themselves give no courage or strength,
and I turn once again to my God.

Tempted to slide back into mud,
down to the bliss of oblivion,
yet I hear the lure of my Lover,
whispering through my story's confusion.
The God who draws me is urging me on,
and I discover my faltering Yes.
I stumble along the rough pathways,
surprised by a hand that is grasping my own.

To and fro, back and forth,
on the twists of the journey,
courage moves me onwards,
faith trusts in the future;
wisdom makes me pause,
I rest by the stream;
taking time to delve deep,
I listen for the Voice.

I reach for the unknown mountain,
to the summit where God speaks anew,
on the boundary of earth and heaven,
the frontier of time and eternity,
the place of a special revealing,
marked by the stones of a cairn.
As I ponder the codes of my dreaming,
I am surprised by the mystery of God.

The hills themselves slowly change,
never as firm as they seem;
shrouded, brooding, and dark,
their rocks splintered by frost,
worn away by the lashing of storms,
no strength in themselves to support me,
only from God comes my help.

With the wind of the Spirit empower me,
stirring the substance of earth,
moving my innermost being,
yet keeping me from all lasting harm.
Keep watch, do not slumber, Guardian of your people,
shade from the heat, healer and guide.
Nourish the life of my truest self,
from this moment on and for ever.

*Deepen my trust in your Presence, my God, for you seem often absent and
hidden, and I am afraid of what the way will bring. Deepen my trust.*

PEACE AND PERPLEXITY

What will become of the city?

Refrain: Lift up your eyes and see:
        the City of all our dreams.

I was glad when my companions of faith
ventured with me to the house of our God.
Weary and tired, yet our feet will stand
within the gates of the City of Peace,
Jerusalem the goal of our longing,
where the pilgrims gather in unity.

Drawn ever closer to the city,
to the place of prayer and of presence,
to faith renewed and hope restored,
to the healing and peace of the Promise,
we your people climb to the gates,
to the seat of your judgment and mercy.

We pray for the peace of Jerusalem.
May those who love you prosper.
Peace be within your walls,
prosperity in all your households.
For the sake of my kindred and friends,
I will pray from my heart for your peace.
For the sake of the house of our God,
I will do all that I can for your good.

*Bless the people of Jerusalem, all who look to Abraham as their ancestor in
faith. Take the energy of our prayers and deeds and transform both place and
people into a city of pilgrimage and peace for the whole world. Bring all of
us there, so that we may taste and see your generous and gracious love.*

DELIGHT AND DEVASTATION

Will I survive the piercing eye?

Refrain: We will not be trapped by the eyes of oppression:
we will see with the eyes of our God.

The haughty look of the powerful,
the contemptuous stare of the wealthy,
the cutting glance of the clever,
the mocking glint of the cowardly:

Burdened by eyes that enslave us,
cast down by eyes of derision,
oppressed by eyes that pursue us,
held fast by eyes that never relent:

The eyes of cameras following us,
the shadow of spies in the dark,
the screen displaying the data,
the silent satellite unseen:

Fiery eyes, angry for justice,
compassionate eyes, warming the poor,
courteous eyes, attentive and waiting,
steady eyes, calm and courageous:

A reverent look awed and still,
a ready glance, willing to obey,
a look of hope, expectant of good,
a look of trust, as between friends.

Fill us with the Spirit of Love, All-Seeing and All-Compassionate God,
that we may look with terrible and kindly eyes on those who oppress us, and
shame them to a change of heart and deed.

DELIVERANCE AND DESTRUCTION

Will we weather the storm?

Refrain: Praise to the God who is for us,
            and for all that is being created.

If you had not been on our side
when destructive powers rose up and barred our path,
if you had not been committed to our good,
like monsters they would have swallowed us alive.

Their anger was kindled against us,
like the sweep of the forest fire.
Their fury bore down upon us,
like the raging torrent in flood,
the waters of chaos that know no limits,
trespassers that are hard to forgive.

Thanks be to you, our deliverer,
you have not given us as prey to their teeth.
We escaped like a bird from the snare of the fowler:
the frame snapped and we have flown free.

In the joy of deliverance we praise you, O God.
Our hearts expand in a new generosity:
we embody the love with which you create.
Even the powers you do not destroy:
you redeem all our failures to live,
you are strong to bring good out of evil.

*In the dangers and risks of the pilgrim way you are with us, our Companion
God. Strengthen us to face the perils of the powers of storm and hunter that
would overwhelm us, and show us again that your creative love is stronger
than anything else in the universe.*

TRUSTWORTHINESS AND TREACHERY

Are we dependable?

Refrain: We trust the Love that never fails,
the God who stands secure.

Those who put their trust in you, O God,
shall be as if they were Mount Zion itself,
rooted in the depths of the earth,
never to be shaken, enduring for ever.

The mountains stand protecting Jerusalem,
city of ramparts and walls that are solid.
So stands our God around the people,
moment by moment, now and for ever.

So may we be constant and true,
giving no sway to the sceptre of wickedness,
establishing the rule of justice in the land,
lest even the righteous be tempted to evil.

Yet our hidden deceits sap the foundations,
masked by the buildings of goodness and courage.
We are wheat and tares indeed for the sifting,
at the place of judgment and mercy.

O God of Truth, give us the spirit of resistance to the subtleties of evil,
insinuating themselves as we grow stronger on the journey. May we be
honest pilgrims, steadfast, trustworthy, and true of heart, rooted only in
your Love.

EXILE AND EXULTATION

Will we come home?

Refrain: Home at last, contented and grateful.

When God takes us home from our exile,
we shall wake from this nightmare and live again.

Bars of iron will be shattered: we shall walk free
from gulag and ghetto, from dungeon and laager.

We shall sing and laugh for joy,
echoed by birdsong and breeze of the spring.

The land itself will rejoice in God,
the whole world give praise for the wonders we have seen.

Lead us home, renew our hope, bring us to life,
like impossible rivers in the cursed and barren desert.

We go on our way sadly, with tears sowing seeds that will die,
we shall return with joy, with gladness bearing our sheaves.

Restore the years, O God, that we have lost, that the locusts have eaten. Give to us the future that we thought we should never see. Make of the present moment a firstfruit of true liberation. Even when we feel exiled, locked in, despairing, move secretly within us and among us, and without our realising it, keep us moving on our journey to your city.

CARE AND CONSUMPTION

How well are we building?

Refrain: Frustrate our schemes and designs,
yet bless us in city and home.

Eternal God, our Rock and our Foundation,
without you all that we build is but rubble.
Blindly and cheaply we construct on sand,
and the buildings subside and crumble.

Those who guard the city do so in vain;
the watchman cannot see the corruption within.
The lights in the towers shine on through the night,
all for vain profit, soon turning to dust.

Foolish we are to rise up so early,
drawn to the work that consumes us.
The bread of anxiety sours and gnaws at us,
we forget you give gifts while we sleep.

Let us turn to our children and play with them,
a glorious waste of mechanical time!
They are our heritage, a gift only from you:
content are those who build steady around them.

Of such buildings is the lasting city made:
blessed are those who delight in such priceless gifts.
They will stand assured when facing their adversaries,
they and their children will grow in stature and wisdom.

Keep us building slowly, steadily, truly. Keep us from being Babel-like,
top-heavy and empty. Keep us building one another up in wisdom and love.
And let us take no anxious thought for tomorrow.

EMBRACE AND EXCLUSION

Do I belong?

*Refrain: From our ancestors to our children's children
let us be grateful for the blessings of home.*

We are blessed if we hold God in awe,
if we walk in the paths of our Creator.
The labour of our hands will bear fruit:
all shall be well, we shall rest content.

Husband and wife will be happy together,
partners and friends will sustain one another:
in intimacy and trust they will embrace,
and gather to tell tales by the fire.

Children will be a blessing round the table,
guests will bring grace to festival times.
As branches of vine and of olive,
each will be God's presence to the other.

We are blessed if we keep the counsels of God,
who dwells in the secret places of our hearts,
who comes to life between us in love,
who shares bread and wine round our hearth.

God will bless us indeed:
we shall have known Jerusalem –
an outpost of the city of peace,
a sign of shalom on the earth.

*Let even the outcast and exile, within us or beyond our gate, not begrudge
the contentment of simple blessings. Let the fortunate open wide their gates
to welcome the outcast and the exile home. In quiet ways may sorrows be
eased and envy dispelled.*

GOLGOTHA AND GENOCIDE

Can faith survive?

Refrain: The litany of lament grows loud and long:
The pulse of faith grows weak.

Does the power of the wicked have no limit?
Why do you not restrain them, O God?
Your people of old knew a measure of affliction,
but they praised you for deeds of deliverance.

Their enemies scored their backs with ploughshares,
opening long furrows of crimson.
But you would not let the adversary prevail,
you cut your people free from the chafing bonds.

Their anger welled up within them,
cursing the enemy with withering scorn:
"May they be as grass that shrivels in the heat,
may they never come to the ripeness of harvest."

An easy exchange it seems to us now,
faced as we are with cruelty unleashed –
exquisite refinements of torture's black arts,
children knifed and dumped in the gutters.

Woe to us when to cleanse means to slaughter,
when genocide seems the simple solution,
when bullets explode into a thousand splinters,
when young and old are abused and discarded.

Why do you not act, mute God, in your justice?
How dare we name you as good any more?
We have entered deep darkness in the midst of the journey,
and the pilgrims are paralyzed, unable to move.

We receive no answer to our prayers, Silent God, and yet still we pray to you
lest we despair. Justify your ways to us, and do not silence us, like Job, with
power and grandeur. Convince us again of·the invincible strength of
vulnerable and crucified love, even when Golgotha and genocide seem worlds
apart. Do not fail us in our extremity.

WATCHING AND WAITING

Dare I enter the dark?

*Refrain: Costing not less than everything,
all manner of things shall be well.*

Empty, exhausted, and ravaged,
in the depths of despair I writhe.
Anguished and afflicted, terribly alone,
I trudge a bleak wasteland, devoid of all love.

In the echoing abyss I call out:
No God of Compassion hears my voice.
Yet still I pray, Open your heart,
for my tears well up within me.

If you keep account of all that drags me down,
there is no way I can ever stand firm.
Paralyzed and powerless, I topple over,
bound by the evil I hate.

But with you is forgivness and grace,
there is nothing I can give – it seems like a death.
The power of your love is so awesome:
I am terrified by your freeing embrace.

Drawn from the murky deeps by a fish hook,
I shout to the air that will kill me:
Must I leave behind all that I cherish
before I can truly breathe free?

Suspended between one world and the next,
I waited for you, my God.
Apprehension and hope struggled within me,
I waited, I longed for your word.

As a watchman waits for the morning,
through the darkest and coldest of nights,
more even than the watchman who peers through the gloom,
I hope for the dawn, I yearn for the light.

You will fulfil your promise to bring me alive,
overflowing with generous love.
You will free me from the grip of evil,
O God of mercy and compassion.

Touching and healing the whole of my being,
you are a God whose reach has no limit.
All that has been lost will one day be found:
the communion of the rescued will rejoice in your name.

Through the dark despairing depths and the drought of the desert, through
the abyss opened up by our failings and folly, we dare to risk our cry to the
living God. For you will not let us escape from our greatest good. In our
struggle with you, fierce, fiery Lover, let some new glory be wrought, and
new and unexpected life come to birth.

CALM AND CONTENTMENT
I shall praise.

Refrain: In quietness and confidence is our strength,
in utter trust our contentment and joy.

Dear God, my heart is not proud,
nor are my eyes haughty.
I do not busy myself in great matters,
nor in what is beyond me.

I am glad I depend on my neighbour,
I make no great claims of my own;
Sealed off by myself I would never know gifts,
never know the bonding of trust.

I have calmed and quietened my whole being,
I am like a child contented at the mother's breast,
in the stillness I look into the eyes of my lover,
I am absorbed in the task of the moment.

It is like the silence of an evening in spring,
made intense by the bleat of a lamb.
It is like the waves of the sea come to rest,
no more than a whisper in the caress of the shore.

The silence and stillness lift the woodsmoke of prayer,
a song of quiet gratitude wafting it high.
Aware of descendants and ancestors with us,
we join the soft chorus of praise.

May we cherish the silence and not be afraid. May we know it not empty
but full of Presence. May the Love at its heart calm our fears. May we know
the gentle touch of a trusting hand.

BEAUTY AND BLISS

I shall wonder.

Refrain: Our gaze is held by your beauty,
            we gasp with wonder and praise.

The splendour of the Ark of the Covenant,
housed in the glory of the Temple,
crowning the City of Peace –
the pilgrims were drawn by the beauty of God.

No wonder that David of old
vowed not to enter his house,
to sleep in the comfort of his bed,
till the ark of the presence found rest.

We are stirred by the festival day,
the ark in triumphal procession,
the people decked out in splendour,
the faithful shouting for joy.

Your covenant with your people is strengthened,
your beauty attracting and leading us on,
to the goodness at the heart of your law,
to the truth brought to life in our deeds.

The beauty of carvings in wood and in stone,
of people transformed in their presence,
the beauty of words and of music,
bring us close to the heart of our God.

Yet more was promised to David that day:
a descendant would inherit the Covenant.
Would we be shown a more lasting beauty,
gloriously embodying the divine and the human?

Refrain: Our gaze is held by your beauty,
we gasp with wonder and praise.

And yet – most wonderful paradox –
the beauty of God touched the outcast:
nothing in the Crucified to delight us,
only to faith's eye is God's glory revealed.

If the ugliest of scars can shine with new light,
if you can fashion new forms from our chaos,
if poets can bring hope from genocide's ashes,
we can rejoice once again in the Beauty of God.

Keep alive in us, Spirit of God, even in desperate days, a vision of a true
and goodly beauty, shaped from the least likely matter of your creation, that
graced and cheered, we may not perish but be encouraged to glory.

LOVING AND LOVED

I shall love.

Refrain: May we be one in the exchanges of love,
in the look of the eyes between lover and loved.

At oases on the pilgrim way we rest together,
sharing the stories and meals that refresh us.
We remember we are called to be holy, not good,
to do what God requires, to delight in God's blessing.

Brothers and sisters, friends of God,
how joyful and pleasant a thing it is –
like the gathering of a mountain range –
when we dwell together in unity.

It is like a precious and fragrant oil,
like the dew of early morning,
or the scent of summer in the forest –
gifts beyond all expectation.

It is like the very beauty of holiness itself,
a sense of Presence in the places of prayer,
the Godward eyes of faithful people,
the times we are surprised by new blessings.

So we give you heartfelt thanks, O God,
that we can glimpse the harmony of humanity,
that we can trust that all creation will be restored,
that all things will be suffused with the light of your glory.

May we hear your gracious invitation, O Triune God, to share the hospi-
tality of your table and the Dance of your Love, and so respond to all that
you have created for us to enjoy.

BLESSING AND BEGINNING

I shall be blessed.

Refrain: Lead us on, Pillar of Flame,
always moving ahead of us.

We your friends and servants bless you, O God,
as we stand by night in your Presence.
We lift up our hands to the holiest of places,
whose walls pray the prayers of the pilgrims.

To the City of Peace we have come at the last,
and give you, our God, our heartfelt praise.
Bless us and all you have given us,
Creator of heaven and of earth.

Bless us as we turn away from the shrines,
lest by lingering we become pillars of salt,
Even the stones will decay into dust:
the Presence will depart from among them.

Absorbing the gifts our ancestors left to us,
we set out once more on our journey.
What we thought was our goal was but a stage on the way,
and the Spirit is urging us on.

Drawn as we may be by Bardsey and Lindisfarne, by Iona and Durham,
by Canterbury and Jerusalem, by Santiago and Rome, let us take courage
from our ancestors of faith, but let us now seek to make holy the places where
we live and to be made holy ourselves by the God who goes on before us.

SMALL AND GREAT, EXILE AND SETTLER, POOR AND WEALTHY

Refrain: Praise to the God who creates us and calls us,
who promises an abundance of blessing.

We praise you, Beloved, we give thanks to your name;
in the loyalty of friendship we give you praise.
In the house where we heard your promises
we give thanks for the blessings of your covenant.
We praise you for you are gracious and courteous,
we sing praise to your name for it is good.
You have chosen us for particular service,
a priestly people whose love is not narrow.

And you are indeed the glorious Creator,
awesome in your freedom and power.
Your will stretches round the great globe,
echoing to the depths of the seas.
You shine through the fierce heat of the sun,
tempered by the tenderness of clouds and rain.
You howl through the winds of the desert,
whilst giving oases of sheltering green.

You yearn for each of us to have a home,
a piece of the earth to cherish and care for.
Your heart goes out to the wandering exile,
in Egypt, in Babylon, in migrants today.
You lived among us a vulnerable child,
fleeing from the wiles of the powers that be.
You know what it means to be cast out of the walls,
yet you prepare a city beyond our imagining.

Fortunate they are who have houses to dwell in,
whose roots reach far in the ground of the past.
Blessed are those with a language of their own,
through which they can hear your marvellous works.

Refrain: Praise to the God who creates us and calls us,
who promises an abundance of blessing.

Inheritors as we are of an ancient story,
we find our place in the greater world.
Through art and music we are consoled and inspired,
through the touch of our neighbour we know we belong.

Let us not fall into the grip of idols,
dazzled by displays of silver and gold.
Let not our wealth feed a monstrous addiction,
growing tall and slowly destroying us.
Let us live from the point of our need,
of the poor, the outcast, the friendless,
the hurt child who lives in us all,
the needy who bring us the gift of your presence.

Let all the first peoples bless you, O God,
aboriginal, in touch with earth's wisdom.
Let the migrant workers bless you, O God,
nomadic in spirit, with no earthly resting place.
Let the settlers on the land bless you, O God,
who husband the earth for its harvest.
Let the powerful bless you, O God,
who hold the earth in their hands.

Creator of the universe, yet friend to each one of us, giving us our homes, yet
planting in us a yearning for a true and lasting city, disturber of the settled
and comforter of the restless wanderer, may we all come together in your
praise.

LOVE WITHOUT END

Refrain: Alleluia! We sing of your love, now and for ever.

We give you thanks, O God, for your goodness,
for your mercies endure for ever.
By solemn promise you are bound to us,
source of grace for ever and ever.

You are the God beyond gods,
a mystery too profound for our thoughts.
In the shadows of the light we discern you,
we are struck by your dazzling darkness.

You reveal the marvels of the universe
to those who listen and patiently look –
from atoms and genes hidden from our eyes
to the shafts of light from long dead stars.

For the beauty of forms ever-changing,
for the slow turning of the sun and the seasons,
for the miracle of the newly born child,
for the rising of our daily bread

At the turning points of our lives you are with us,
through times of bewildering change.
At the crossing of the boundaries of the known
by strangers and dreams you encourage us.

You rescue us from slavery and exile,
you are with us on our desert journey,
you give us a place we can cherish,
where the vulnerable find their protection.

You have given us our parts in the story,
from our ancestors whose names are forgotten
to our descendants whose names are not known,
to each a new name in your presence.

Refrain: Alleluia! We sing of your love, now and for ever.

You gave of yourself in the one called Jeshua,
showing us the way of dying to live;
you renewed the gifts of your Spirit,
your glory has shone through your saints.

In you we are bound to one another,
linked by threads seen and unseen,
destined for love in eternity,
when all that has decayed is restored.

*In contemplation, discernment, and endurance may we take into the
presence of God all that is intractable and unresolved in the life of this planet
and its peoples — and in our own lives also — until the time comes when the
Spirit of gratitude will spread over all things and for all that has been we
shall indeed give our thanks, and to all that shall be we shall sing our Yes.*

BY THE WATERS OF BABYLON

*Refrain: Blessed are those who hunger and strive
for all that is just and good.*

By the waters of Babylon we sat down and wept
when we remembered the smouldering city.
We hid our harps in the thickets of the willow;
silently and bitterly we grieved.

They who drove us captive from our homeland
demanded of us a song of our joy.
Goaded by their torment we cried out,
"Sing the Lord's praise in a strange land?
How can we throw our pearls before swine?
You trample on our name, you rob us of hope,
we cannot betray what is holy and precious.
To proclaim what is intimate is to lose it for ever."

It is hard to be faithful and firm,
as despair overwhelms us in torrents.
Troubled we are and uncertain,
no longer assured of God's presence.
O God, do you hear the cries of our hearts
now that we are so far from your city?
On foreign soil can we worship you still?
Have you withdrawn from us for ever?

Yet if I forget you, Jerusalem,
may the hand that plucks the harp wither.
May my tongue cleave to the roof of my mouth
if I do not give Jerusalem my heart's desire.

Refrain: Blessed are those who hunger and strive
for all that is just and good

Great anger rises within me, a thirst for revenge
against those who have destroyed the city.
Even our kin wanted Jerusalem ruined,
stripped bare to its very foundations.
Colonial power and neighbouring tribe
laid us waste with their scorn and their greed.
"May your cities be burnt to a cinder,
your children dashed to pieces on the rocks."

O God, hear the honesty in my rage,
the sharp pain in my heart.
To you alone can I trust the hatred I feel,
knowing you will use it for good.
But how? What to do with my anger?
For its power I need: it must not be taken from me.
"We who have lost so much, hear us.
We who have been so much abused, hear us.
We who now live on the margins, hear us.
We who are denied our own language, hear us."

Yet truly their life has no meaning,
their hearts as hollow as their mockery.
They destroy themselves by their cruelty,
they become as the dust of the city they destroyed.
No, do not let them vanish for ever,
but shame them to repentance and justice.

Work in us all the deeds of your grace.
May we restrain our furious desires,
refusing to be dragged down to their mire.
But keep us from too easy a kindness.
With patient tenacity may we endure,
and keep our anger alive.

Create a new heart in all who oppress,
break down the structures that bind them.
So you will give us the sign that we need
for the grace at the last to forgive.
For now let us mightily strive with our enemies,
until all of us, limping, are blessed.
Together may we sing a new song
as we build a more glorious city.

As cracks split the walls of the houses of prayer,
as the faiths are compromised by collusion with oppression,
as we betray you by killing one another in your name,
as the Spirit of the ages moves on,
challenge us again, Mysterious God,
in homeland or in exile,
in delving within, expecting to be changed,
in anger and truth changing the world,
that we may see beyond the convictions
with which we bind and cage both you and one another,
and having seen, may act.
As no stone was left standing on another in Jerusalem,
so it will be in Canterbury and Rome.
They will fall because their vision is too narrow.
May we not rebuild them as of old,
but keep them as empty silent spaces
that they may speak to us eloquently of what is beyond us.
Empower us to build the City of Peace wherever we are.
May we discern your call to protect and shape
city and home, farm and wilderness, body and community,
all in harmony with your will.
May they alone become temples of your presence,
the places of our prayer,
and the new Jerusalem for which we dream and long.

GOD'S GENTLE TOUCH

Refrain: To those we barely notice
God draws especially close.

Homeless and restless, I sleep on the streets,
huddled in the doorway of the jeweller's store.
Why are they afraid of me who can do them no harm?
Why do they all pass hurriedly by?

A woman stops, eyes steady and clear:
her hand clasps mine, enclosing a coin.
She speaks a few words, spends a few seconds,
risking the laughter of those who pass by.

A man draws close with hesitant step,
embarrassed and awkward when faced with the strange.
Yet he stays long enough to give me some broth,
a waste in the thoughts of those who pass by.

The crypt of a church lies dusty, unused,
till a few catch a vision of a haven of care.
There are some who give food with a listening ear,
a hope unknown to those who pass by.

A few with pure hearts among those who are wealthy
keep stirring the conscience of people with power,
pressing for the changes that justice requires,
sword in the path of those who pass by.

Do they give me a glimpse of an unusual God?
Is there glory in the costly giving of self?
Am I the one God especially loves?
Is God far from those who pass by?

The skilled and the powerful think they are favoured,
they call on their God to buttress their pride.
They miss the gentleness of a touch that is loving,
fearful hands push away and of course they pass by.

We give you thanks, surprising God, with all our hearts. Through the Poor Man of Nazareth who embodied your love, and whose Spirit inspires us still, you keep alive the hope that the true strength of the gentle and merciful will overcome the brittle force of the fearful and powerful, that at the last the unrecognized will indeed inherit the earth.

LIGHT OF LIGHT

Refrain: Always aware of us,
ever-present with us,
ceaselessly creating us—
we respond in love,
we tremble and adore,
our God, mysterious and faithful.

Light of light, you have searched me out and known me.
You know where I am and where I go,
you see my thoughts from afar.
You discern my paths and my resting places,
you are acquainted with all my ways.
Yes, and not a word comes from my lips
but you, O God, have heard it already.
You are in front of me and you are behind me,
you have laid your hand on my shoulder.
Such knowledge is too wonderful for me,
so great that I cannot fathom it.

Where shall I go from your Spirit,
where shall I flee from your Presence?
If I climb to the heavens you are there:
if I descend to the depths of the earth, you are there also.
If I spread my wings towards the morning,
and fly to the uttermost shores of the sea,
even there your hand will lead me,
and your right hand will hold me.
If I should cry to the darkness to cover me,
and the night to enclose me,
the darkness is no darkness to you,
and the night is as clear as the day.

For you have created every part of my being,
cell and tissue, blood and bone.
You have woven me in the womb of my mother;
I will praise you, so wonderfully am I made.
Awesome are your deeds and marvellous are your works.
You know me to the very core of my being;
nothing in me was hidden from your eyes
when I was formed in silence and secrecy,
in intricate splendour in the depths of the earth.
Even as they were forming you saw my limbs,
each part of my body shaped by your finger.

How deep are your thoughts to me, O God,
how great is the sum of them.
Were I to count them they are more in number
than the grains of sand upon the sea-shore –
and still I would know nothing about you –
yet still would you hold me in the palm of your hand.

Yet my trust falters. I see all that is wrong in the world and in my heart, all
the mutual loathing and hatreds, all the betrayals and lies. Scour our hearts,
refine our thoughts, strengthen our wills, guide us in your Way.

AGAINST EVILDOERS

Those who defraud the poor of their pensions,
those who deprive the poor of their land,
those who grow wealthy on the backs of the poor:

God of justice and power,
restrain them, confine them, bring them to their knees.

Those who have no coins for the meter,
those who walk far for their fuel,
those whose backs are bent low,

God of compassion and power,
rescue them, liberate them, lift up their hearts.

Those who fly flags of convenience,
those who pollute the rivers and streams,
those who release acid to clouds,

God of justice and power,
restrain them, confine them, bring them to their knees.

Those who sweat in the engine rooms,
those whose health is damaged by their work,
dwellers in forests where the leaves shrivel,

God of compassion and power,
rescue them, liberate them, lift up their hearts.

Those who trade in drugs that destroy,
those who smuggle arms that recoil on their makers,
governments who cynically collude,

God of justice and power,
restrain them, confine them, bring them to their knees.

Those with poison in their veins,
those who will never walk again,
people deprived of their rights,

God of compassion and power,
rescue them, liberate them, lift up their hearts.

Those who with malice slander their neighbours,
those who twist words for the sake of a scandal,
those who use words to boost their esteem,

God of justice and power,
restrain them, confine them, bring them to their knees.

Those who are deprived of their name,
those without value or worth,
those who know not their own language,

God of compassion and power,
rescue them, liberate them, lift up their hearts.

Those who beat the young to submission,
those who torture and rape,
those who violate their children,

God of justice and power,
restrain them, confine them, bring them to their knees.

Children who cower in fear,
all who are wounded and scarred,
survivors who twist in the darkness,

God of compassion and power,
rescue them, liberate them, lift up their hearts.

With the psalmist our anger rises at the harm we human beings cause one
another. We cry out for the oppressed and defenceless — Let the arrogant and
mighty crumble under the weight of their own evil! Let them be plunged into
the quaking mire! Let burning coals rain down on their heads! Let them be
hunted to an exhausted and terror-struck end! Bring them to their knees at
the last, restrained, confined, powerless to harm, at the mercy of those they
have wronged.

IMPOSSIBLE DREAM?

Refrain: Stretched between anguish and joy,
we live the paradox of faith.

My whole being reaches towards you, my God:
my heart yearns for your welcoming love.
I would run to embrace you as to a friend,
my voice leaping and singing for joy.

Like incense my prayer rises to meet you,
carried on the breath from my lungs.
My arms stretch out, lifting me high,
seeking the hand that is eager to touch.

To the unheard music my feet start dancing;
embodied in movement I become as my joy.
From the depths of my belly arises a cry,
a glorious Yes to the whole of my life.

O that it were so! It is only a dream,
far from the walls of this imprisoning cell.
Exhausted and limp, I stagger and fall,
my prayer no more than a flickering thought.

Silenced by the greedy and scared,
I have no one to utter a passionate cry,
the heartfelt anguish of the unjustly imprisoned,
from the narrow cells underground.

I scratch my name on the prison wall,
frightened I am losing all sense of my being.
Will no one speak on behalf of the mute,
will not the Judge of the earth do right?

Is the hope of my heart an impossible dream?
Will I ever dance in the rays of the sun?
Will I know the warmth of a welcoming hand?
Will a voice of love ever call me by name?

May the fitful tremblings of our prayer move through the world with compassion to give to someone in prison, neglected and forgotten, at least a moment's respite from despair.

TRUST THOUGH REJECTED

Refrain: Alone and rejected dare I trust,
hearing only the Silence of God?

I call to you, my God, with heartfelt cry:
insistent in my need, I seek your Presence.
Barely do I believe and yet still do I pray,
and make no secret of all my troubles.

When my voice croaks and is faint,
when weariness overtakes me on the way,
do you hear my whisper and know where I walk?
Do you know there is much that makes me stumble?

I am left in the silence with no one to help me,
not even a hand draws close to touch me.
I can no longer speak, I drift in a vacuum,
thick glass hems me in: no one can see me.

With a cry without words or sounds,
I search for your Presence, O God.
Do you still have the power to rescue me?
Do you care enough for my plight?

Save me from all that oppresses me,
from the powers that are too strong for me.
Lift me from the dungeon that confines me,
that I may laugh and sing again.

With generous heart beyond measure,
will you come to my healing and rescue?
Then I shall rejoice in the voices of praise,
and give you the glory for ever.

Rejected and isolated, we seek warmth and affirmation, nourishment and
good company. Come with the wind and the bread, the water and the word,
the fire and the balm.

AFRAID OF DEATH

Refrain: Dissolving into the void,
disintegrating to dust,
I cry out in desperate need,
Deliver me from the fear of death.

My heart is open, I come without guile,
I dare to pray to a God who is faithful.
I cannot justify myself in your Presence;
with trembling I bring my desperate need.
I make no plea for justice,
I depend on your mercy and grace.

The devourer is crushing my bones,
the ravenous hounds knock me to the ground.
the unconscious dark overshadows me;
dumped in the ditch I am given up for dead.
My will to live grows faint within me,
my heart is appalled and terrified.
No longer does the stream flow through me:
my taste is of death, acrid and dry

I cling to the memories of faith,
my heart once lifted in gratitude.
When I least expected your presence,
with the deepest joy you surprised me.
Let me be calm and reflect on your goodness,
on the innumerable gifts you have given me.

Refrain: Dissolving into the void,
disintegrating to dust,
I cry out in desperate need,
Deliver me from the fear of death.

Trembling I stretch out my hands,
hungry for the food that sustains.
Without you I cannot but perish,
starved in the depths of my being.
Long have I believed you are with me,
however unaware I become.
Do not sever the threads that connect us,
lest I drift into space for ever.

Let me hear of your compassion and mercy,
rising with the warmth of the sun.
Show me the way I should travel,
your kindly Spirit giving me courage.
Deliver me from the shades of death;
for the sake of your name calm me.

Release the grip of the power of death,
disarm all those who oppress me.
May death and death-dealers have no meaning,
shrivelled to dust and transfigured to joy.

Like the disciples of old, we are afraid of the power of the storm that destroys
and terrified of the power of the love that transfigures. May we hear again
the accents of encouragement: Do not be afraid, be of good courage, I am
with you.

THE CREATOR LOVER

Refrain: O Lover, Divine and Human,
intimate, insistent, and tender,
courteous in paying attention,
passionate in wholehearted embrace,
bring us alive and alight,
each a singular creation.

Blessed be you, O God our Creator:
you are the source of our power and skill,
you teach our hands to shape chaos,
our fingers to mould intractable clay.
You swive with us in a dance of delight,
creating what is new with your partners.

We seem to ourselves to be but a breath,
our days a shadow that soon passes by,
insignificant in the vastness of space.
But O the wonder and marvel of your touch –
awesome that you should draw so near,
embracing, empowering the children of earth.

You bring us alive with electrifying power,
you touch us with the fork of lightning.
Flesh and blood can hardly contain you,
yet your power does not destroy us.
At the heart of the flame is a tender calm,
in courtesy you never intrude.
Little by little you warm us to life,
and we take part in the work of creation.

Refrain: O Lover, Divine and Human,
intimate, insistent, and tender,
courteous in paying attention,
passionate in wholehearted embrace,
bring us alive and alight,
each a singular creation.

You strive with evil, with destructive powers,
not with the matching of strength,
but absorbing their harm in your dying,
in the expending of love and of life.
Hold us steady when we are faced with chaos and fear,
when the waters foam and rage through the night,
that we may pierce to the eye of the storm,
and know the love that sustains.

So we shall sing a new song,
on flute and trumpet singing your praise.
We and our children shall be people of beauty,
burgeoning with life, maturing to vintage.
The earth will produce in abundance,
the sheep will lamb in their thousands,
there will be no distress of miscarriage,
no loud lamentation in our streets.

Creator Spirit, surge through us with the thunder of the pounding waves,
breathe through us with the whisper of the evening breeze, dance through us
with the leaping flames of the sun, ripple through us with the merriment of
the mountain stream.

REGULAR BLESSINGS

Refrain: *The rhythm of the drums,*
the beat of the heart,
reliable and steady,
the voice of your faithfulness.

For the dawning of the light,
for the sun at mid-day,
for the shade of the evening,
we give thanks to our God.

For the rising of the moon,
for the guiding stars,
for the comets on cue,
we give thanks to our God.

For the breaking of the fast,
for noontide's refreshment,
for the meal round the table,
we give thanks to our God.

For the greening of the woodland,
for the grains of the harvest,
for the fruits in their season,
we give thanks to our God.

For the cry of the baby,
for the flowering of youth,
for the strength of maturity,
we give thanks to our God.

For laws that protect us,
for those on alert,
for the routines of safety,
we give thanks to our God.

Refrain: The rhythm of the drums,
　　　the beat of the heart,
　　　reliable and steady,
　　　the voice of your faithfulness.

For the fall of the autumn,
for the quiet of winter,
for the boundary of death,
we give thanks to our God.

For the trust of friends,
for the blessings of home,
for the covenants of love,
we give thanks to our God.

For the unfailingly generous,
for the wisdom of years,
for constant compassion,
we give thanks to our God.

For the hidden who serve us,
for the water and power,
for work taken for granted,
we give thanks to our God.

God of good gifts, surprise us again with how reliable you are. Thank you
for the trustworthiness of so many people in their repeated tasks for the benefit
of the whole community. We touch a mystery unsearchable and wonderful,
the marvel of the everyday. And you, O God, are constant and faithful,
abundant in steadfast love, passionate and limitless in the giving of yourself
to us and all the world, partners as we are in your covenant of creation.

SOCIETY RESTORED

Justice and Jerusalem

Refrain: Praise to the God of Justice and Peace:
from the depth of our being we praise you.

We praise you, God beyond gods;
with a world restored we praise you.
In faith we anticipate that day,
and praise you for the firstfruits of its coming.

We do not put our trust in passing fashions,
nor in the promises of powerful people.
They are powerless to save, their ashes are scattered,
their words soon crumbling to dust.

To the Creator of the infinite heavens,
of the earth and the seas and their creatures,
who works unceasingly for justice,
we give our heartfelt praise.

You keep faith with your promises for ever,
you put right the wrongs of the oppressed.
You give food to the hungry and thirsty,
you set the captives free.

You give sight to the blind,
your arms lift up those who are bowed down,
you love those who live simply,
you care for the stranger, the widowed, the orphan.

At times we do these things with you,
surprising ourselves by our courage,
giving voice to those who are not heard,
troubling and pressing the makers of policy.

Refrain: Praise to the God of Justice and Peace:
  from the depths of our being we praise you.

The cities we know are a patchwork,
a jostling of places of hope and despair.
Yet still we give thanks for the vision
of the City of Harmony and Peace.

In the justice of relationships made right,
in the peace that is well-being for all,
we worship the God of justice and peace,
we praise the God of freedom and joy,
we adore the God of love and new life,
we bless the God of reconciliation and healing,
we glorify the God of harmony and bliss.
We add our voice to the music of God;
we fall silent in the presence of Mystery,
in wonder and awe and love,
the Mystery that is the Source of our being
and the Goal of our longing,
beautiful, utterly holy, glorious light,
unbounded love: Alleluia! Alleluia!

PROMISES FULFILLED
City and Countryside

Refrain: Praise God whose Promise is fulfilled:
it gives us great joy to give thanks.

The earth itself is transformed,
the City of Peace is established:
creatures in their thousands leap for joy,
and the people dance in the streets.

The scattered outcasts greet one another,
kings and clowns tumble together,
the hobbling teach the dancers new steps,
the scars of the wounded shine.

The torn hills heal over with grass,
the gnarled trees put forth new shoots.
Ramblers and farmers take care of the land,
the scattered homesteads dwell in safety.

Protesters and politicians sit down together,
the clever sit at the feet of the wise.
The frantic are calmed by those in wheelchairs,
the sexually diverse are welcomed in love.

The cattle are released from their pens,
the hens run free from their sheds.
The walls of the camps are demolished,
numbers are forgotten and names are restored.

No longer do we glory in the might of our arms,
taking pride in the weapons we polish.
No more is the tallest and biggest the best;
no one even thinks of trampling the weak.

Refrain: Praise God whose Promise is fulfilled:
it gives us great joy to give thanks.

Women and men bring their gifts to each other;
no longer are they driven to harm and abuse.
In eyes that speak truth they see each other,
and know how to touch in the sparkling of love.

Marvellous rarities are tasted by all,
bread that is wholesome is baked once again.
The water we drink springs clear from the hills,
the finest wines grace every table.

The skaters spiral on the frozen lakes,
the skiers exult on the mountain slopes,
the gliders swoop and soar through the skies,
the surfers ride the thunder of the waves.

Through the artists a world of bliss is unveiled,
through the poets fresh images of truth are revealed,
through the scientist what is hidden comes to the light,
through the lovers unfolds the joy of new life.

Restored, fulfilled, gathered together,
we know we belong to the universe.
In songs of harmony we embrace one another,
transfigured in the Presence of the One who is All.

In the celebration that embraces the exile and outcast,
in the joy that sings of freedom at last,
we worship the God of justice and peace,
we praise the God of freedom and joy,
we adore the God of love and new life,
we bless the God of reconciliation and healing,
we glorify the God of harmony and bliss.
We add our voice to the music of God;
we fall silent in the presence of Mystery,
in wonder and awe and love,
the Mystery that is the Source of our being
and the Goal of our belonging,
beautiful, utterly holy, glorious light,
unbounded love. Alleluia! Alleluia!

CREATION RENEWED

Touched and Transfigured

Refrain: Praise to the transfiguring God,
whose touch transforms and renews.

Let the Alleluias ring out in the dark,
the darkness that dazzles with unfathomable light.
Let the People of the Way sing their praise,
alive in the Communion and Mystery of Love.

The Lover, the Beloved, the Spirit Between,
the Love that cannot but be outpoured,
pulsing, cherishing, urging new life,
astonishing, wonderful, marvellous to see.

The threads binding together this extraordinary love
are gossamer and golden, invisible and strong,
reaching out to connect all creation for ever,
from amoeba to human, from atom to brain.

So diverse and complex is this web that we share,
so many forms to name and delight in,
we needs must choose to focus our praise,
our voices finding words for those who are silent.

Let the sun and the moon and the stars
and the earth and the ocean give praise.
We are bound with them; they belong with us:
all change – must it be to decay?

The mountains levelled to plains are changed;
the oceans bed buckles to rise from the sea;
the rivers carry silt and make the vales fertile,
the snows melt to release the spring.

Refrain: Praise to the transfiguring God,
whose touch transforms and renews.

Seeds yield their life in the darkness of earth,
the flowers, the fruits, and the grains all grow;
some change in the earth to be seen only at harvest,
their abundance deepening our sense of well-being.

The worms and the parasites, hidden from view,
all work their mysterious ways,
puzzling destruction a prelude to life,
a transformation that stuns us to silence.

All is changed and may seem to be lost,
and we too know death and decline.
Yet working within us, unnoticed, unseen,
is the thread that binds and transforms.

And we touch one another to pain and to pleasure,
our skin so vulnerable, so finely tuned.
Can we reach out and create life with our God?
Can we lose yet discover ourselves?

What once was a curse can become a wise wound,
the hand that abused can caress and be kind,
violation can change to the sharing of passion,
we can be warmed to life by an intimate fire.

Praise, praise above all,
all that is No is transformed into Yes,
Yes to the God in whom we belong,
belong together in the dance of delight.

In the love that has taken and shaped every power,
in the new creation that rises from the totally dead,
we worship the God of justice and peace,
we praise the God of freedom and joy,
we adore the God of love and new life,
we bless the God of reconciliation and healing,
we glorify the God of harmony and bliss.
We add our voice to the music of God;
we fall silent in the presence of Mystery,
in wonder and awe and love,
the Mystery that is the Source of our being
and the Goal of our longing,
beautiful, utterly holy, glorious light,
unbounded love. Alleluia! Alleluia!

RECONCILIATION EMBRACED
Held and Healed

Refrain: Praise to the God who overcomes all divisions,
who bears the pain of our healing.

Blessed are those who refuse to take vengeance,
blessed are those who cause no harm,
blessed are those who break the cycles of slaughter,
blessed are those who bless and do not curse.

Blessed are those who resist the temptations of power,
who refuse to gather it to themselves.
Blessed are the little ones who find new courage
to claim and inhabit their own.

Blessed are those who seek to reconcile,
who themselves form a bridge for strange meetings.
Blessed are those who repent of their oppression,
blessed are the harmed who show them mercy.

Blessed are those who absorb others' hurts,
who refuse to give back in like manner.
Blessed are those who keep in touch with their enemies,
who refuse to let them go.

Blessed are the judges who wisely discern,
who help to put right what is wrong,
who bring together those who are estranged,
at no little cost to themselves.

Blessed are those who use the sword as a scalpel,
to be accurate and clear in their telling of truth,
who protect and probe but do not destroy,
whose wounds serve only to purify and prune.

Blessed is the One who bears the world's pain,
who loves and endures to the end,
who holds to the heart a wincing world,
who surprises us with healing and hope.

In the reconciliation that is based on repentance and mercy,
in the healing that has held and enfolded the pain,
we worship the God of justice and peace,
we praise the God of freedom and joy,
we adore the God of love and new life,
we bless the God of reconciliation and healing,
we glorify the God of harmony and bliss.
We add our voice to the music of God;
we fall silent in the presence of Mystery,
in wonder and awe and love,
the Mystery that is the Source of our being
and the Goal of our longing,
beautiful, utterly holy, glorious light,
unbounded love. Alleluia! Alleluia!

HARMONY CELEBRATED

Sounds and Silence

Refrain: Praise to the Creator of harmony,
            in the music of silence and sound.

We praise you, O God, holy and beloved!
We praise you for your glory and wisdom!
We praise you for your creative power!
We praise you for your deeds of deliverance!

We praise you in a glorious symphony!
We praise you on the flute and harp!
We praise you with the caress of the trumpet!
We praise you with the solace of the cello!

We praise you on the quickening horn!
We praise you on the strumming guitar!
We praise you with the pipes of the clans!
We praise you on the deep resounding drums!

We praise you in the unnoticed pauses
that make music of disordered sounds!
We praise you in the depths of the silence,
in the music of the dance between eyes that love!

We praise you for all your gifts!
We praise you for your mysterious being!
We praise you for weaving us together!
We praise you that we belong to the universe!

Let everything that breathes under the sun,
let the voices of our ancestors of old,
let worlds unknown, within and beyond,
all on this glad day give you praise!

In the music that is wrought from the silence,
in the silence where we hear the quietest of echoes,
we worship the God of justice and peace,
we praise the God of freedom and joy,
we adore the God of love and new life,
we bless the God of reconciliation and healing,
we glorify the God of harmony and bliss.
We add our voice to the music of God;
we fall silent in the presence of Mystery,
in wonder and awe and love,
the Mystery that is the Source of our being
and the Goal of our longing,
beautiful, utterly holy, glorious light,
unbounded love. Alleluia! Alleluia!